Popular Dance

From Ballroom to Hip-Hop

Karen Lynn Smith

Consulting editor:
Elizabeth A. Hanley,
Associate Professor
Emerita of Kinesiology,
Penn State University

☑Checkmark Books®
An imprint of Infobase Publishing

Popular Dance: From Ballroom to Hip-Hop

Copyright © 2010 by Infobase Publishing

Checkmark Books
An imprint of Infobase Publishing
132 West 31st Street
New York NY 10001

ISBN-10: 1-60413-977-3
ISBN-13: 978-1-60413-977-8

The Library of Congress has cataloged the hardcover edition of this work as follows:

Library of Congress Cataloging-in-Publication Data
Smith, Karen Lynn
  Popular dance : from ballroom to hip-hop / Karen Lynn Smith.
    p. cm. — (World of dance)
  Includes bibliographical references and index.
  ISBN 978-1-60413-484-1 (hardcover)
  1. Dance—Juvenile literature. I. Title. II. Series.
  GV1596.5.S55 2010
  793.3—dc22   2009053491

Checkmark books are available at special discounts when purchased in bulk quantities for businesses, associations, institutions, or sales promotions. Please call our Special Sales Department in New York at (212) 967-8800 or (800) 322-8755.

You can find Chelsea House on the World Wide Web at
http://www.chelseahouse.com

Text design by Kerry Casey
Cover design by Alicia Post
Composition by EJB Publishing Services
Cover printed by Bang Printing, Brainerd, MN
Book printed and bound by Bang Printing, Brainerd, MN
Date printed: June 2010
Printed in the United States of America

10 9 8 7 6 5 4 3 2 1

This book is printed on acid-free paper.

All links and Web addresses were checked and verified to be correct at the time of publication. Because of the dynamic nature of the Web, some addresses and links may have changed since publication and may no longer be valid.

CONTENTS

INTRODUCTION

The world of dance is yours to enjoy! Dance has existed from time immemorial. It has been an integral part of celebrations and rituals, a means of communication with gods and among humans, and a basic source of enjoyment and beauty.

Dance is a fundamental element of human behavior and has evolved over the years from primitive movement of the earliest civilizations to traditional cultural or folk styles, to the classical ballet and modern dance genres popular today. The term *dance* is broad and, therefore, not limited to the genres noted above. In the twenty-first century, dance includes ballroom, jazz, tap, aerobics, and a myriad of other movement activities. The joy derived from participating in dance of any genre and the physical activity required provide the opportunity for the pursuit of a healthy lifestyle in today's world.

The richness of cultural traditions observed in the cultural, or folk, dance genre offers the participant, as well as the spectator, insight into the customs, geography, dress, and religious nature of a particular people. Originally passed on from one generation to the next, many cultural, or folk, dances continue to evolve as our civilization and society change. From these quaint beginnings of traditional dance, a new genre emerged as a way to appeal to the upper level of society: ballet. This new form of dance rose quickly in popularity and remains so today. The genre of cultural, or folk, dance continues to be an important part of ethnic communities throughout the United States, particularly in large cities.

When the era of modern dance emerged as a contrast and a challenge to the rigorously structured world of ballet, it was not readily accepted as an art form. Modern dance was interested in the communication of emotional experiences—through basic movement, as well as uninhibited movement—not through the academic tradition of ballet masters. Modern dance, however, found its aficionados and is a popular art form today.

No dance form is permanent, definitive, or ultimate. Changes occur, but the basic element of dance endures. Dance is for all people. One need only recall that dance needs neither common race nor common language for communication; it has been, and remains, a universal means of communication.

The one fact that each reader should remember is that dance has always been, and always will be, a form of communication. This is its legacy to the world.

***

In *Popular Dance: From Ballroom to Hip-Hop*, author Karen Lynn Smith invites readers to discover the myriad of popular dances and their roles in society from the advent of the "dancing master" of the fifteenth and sixteenth centuries to the present day. Because dance has always been an integral part of society throughout the world, Smith incorporates the cultural and political aspects that have influenced, and continue to influence, the world of dance.

Dances of the Renaissance, Baroque period, and Victorian era are described in detail for the reader; the broad influence of European dance in the early British colonies in America (from East to West) is included along with Native American dance—both Indian and Hawaiian. The early twentieth century, with its wide variety of dances, is characterized by obvious social and cultural changes, due in part to the role of dance at this time. In the mid-twentieth century, dances were influenced by World War II, Hollywood, jazz, and the big band sound, although the square dance and other folk styles remained a part of our culture.

From the late twentieth century to the present day, dance has "exploded" in many respects. Smith presents the many changes and adaptations in dance from the advent of rock 'n' roll to the promotion of dance videos for health to the possibility of DanceSport's (competitive ballroom dance) becoming part of a future Olympic Games program.

—Elizabeth A. Hanley
Associate Professor Emerita of Kinesiology at
Pennsylvania State University

FOREWORD

In song and dance, man expresses himself as a member of
a higher community. He forgets how to walk and speak
and is on the way into flying into the air, dancing. . . .
His very gestures express enchantment.

—Friedrich Nietzsche

In a conversation with George Balanchine [one of the twentieth century's most famous choreographers and the cofounder of the New York City Ballet] discussing the definition of dance, we evolved the following description: "Dance is an expression of time and space, using the control of movement and gesture to communicate."

Dance is central to the human being's expression of emotion. Every time we shake someone's hand, lift a glass in a toast, wave good-bye, or applaud a performer, we are doing a form of dance. We live in a universe of time and space, and dance is an art form invented by human beings to express and convey emotions. Dance is profound.

There are melodies that, when played, will cause your heart to droop with sadness for no known reason. Or a rousing jig or mazurka will have your foot tapping in an accompanying rhythm, seemingly beyond your control. The emotions, contacted through music, spur the body to react physically. Our bodies have just been programmed to express emotions. We dance for many reasons: for religious rituals from the most ancient times; for dealing with sadness, tearfully swaying and holding hands at a wake; for celebrating weddings, joyfully spinning in circles; for entertainment; for dating and mating. How many millions of couples through the ages have said, "We met at a dance"? But most of all, we dance for joy, often exclaiming, "How I love to dance!" Oh, the JOY OF DANCE!

I was teaching dance at a boarding school for emotionally disturbed children, ages 9 through 16. They were participating with 20 other schools in the National Dance Institute's (NDI) year-round program. The boarding school children had been traumatized in frightening and mind-boggling ways. There were a dozen students in my class, and the average attention span may have been 15 seconds—which made for a raucous bunch. This was a tough class.

One young boy, an 11-year-old, was an exception. He never took his eyes off of me for the 35 minutes of the dance class, and they were blazing blue eyes—electric, set in a chalk-white face. His body was slim, trim, superbly proportioned, and he stood arrow-straight. His lips were clamped in a rigid, determined line as he learned and executed every dance step with amazing skill. His concentration was intense despite the wild cavorting, noise, and otherwise disruptive behavior supplied by his fellow classmates.

At the end of class, I went up to him and said, "Wow, can you dance. You're great! What's your name?"

Those blue eyes didn't blink. Then he parted his rigid lips and bared his teeth in a grimace that may have been a smile. He had a big hole where his front teeth should be. I covered my shock and didn't let it show. Both top and bottom incisors had been worn away by his continual grinding and rubbing of them together. One of the supervisors of the school rushed over to me and said, "Oh, his name is Michael. He's very intelligent, but he doesn't speak."

I heard Michael's story from the supervisor. Apparently, when he was a toddler in his playpen, he witnessed his father shooting his mother; then putting the gun to his own head, the father killed himself. It was close to three days before the neighbors broke in to find the dead and swollen bodies of his parents. The dehydrated and starving little boy was stuck in his playpen, sitting in his own filth. The orphaned Michael disappeared into the foster care system, eventually ending up in the boarding school. No one had ever heard him speak.

In the ensuing weeks of dance class, I built and developed choreography for Michael and his classmates. In the spring, they were scheduled to dance in a spectacular NDI show called *The Event of the Year*. At the boarding school, I used Michael as the leader and as a model for the others and began welding all of the kids together, inventing a vigorous and energetic dance to utilize their explosive energy. It took awhile, but they were coming together, little by little over the months. And through all that time, the best in the class—the determined and concentrating Michael—never spoke.

That spring, dancers from the 22 different schools with which the NDI had dance programs were scheduled to come together at Madison Square Garden for *The Event of the Year*. There would be more than 2,000 dancers, a symphony orchestra, a jazz orchestra, a chorus, Broadway stars, narrators, and Native American Indian drummers. There was scenery that was the length of an entire city block and visiting guest children from six foreign countries coming to dance with our New York City children. All of these elements had to come together and fit into a spectacular performance, with only one day of rehearsal. The foremost challenge was how to get 2,000 dancing children on stage for the opening number.

At NDI, we have developed a system called "the runs." First, we divide the stage into a grid with colored lines making the outlines of box shapes, making a mosaic of patterns and shapes on the stage floor. Each outlined box holds a class from one of the schools, which consists of 15 to 30 children. Then, we add various colored lines as tracks, starting offstage and leading to the boxes. The dancers line up in the wings, hallways, and various holding areas on either side of the stage. At the end of the overture, they burst onto the stage, running and leaping and following their colored tracks to their respective boxes, where they explode into the opening dance number.

We had less than three minutes to accomplish "the runs." It's as if a couple of dozen trains coming from different places and traveling on different tracks all arrived at a station at the same time, safely pulling into their allotted spaces. But even before starting, it would take us almost an hour just to get the dancers lined up in the correct holding areas offstage, ready to make their entrance. We had scheduled one shot to rehearse the opening. It had to work the first time, or we would have to repeat everything. That would mean going into overtime at a great expense.

I gave the cue to start the number. The orchestra, singers, lights, and stagehands all commenced on cue, and the avalanche of 2,000 children was let loose on their tracks. "The runs" had begun!

After about a minute, I realized something was wrong. There was a big pileup on stage left, and children were colliding into each other and bunching up behind some obstacle. I ran over to discover the source of the problem: Michael and his classmates. He had ignored everything and led the group from his school right up front, as close to the audience as he could get. Inspiring his dancing buddies, they were a crew of leaping, contorting demons—dancing up a storm, but blocking some 600 other dancers trying to get through.

I rushed up to them, yelling, "You're in the wrong place! Back up! Back up!"

Michael—with his eyes blazing, mouth open, and legs and arms spinning in dance movements like an eggbeater—yelled out, "Oh, I am so happy! I am so happy! Thank you, Jacques! Oh, it's so good! I am so happy!"

I backed off, stunned into silence. I sat down in the first row of the audience and was joined by several of the supervisors, teachers, and chaperones from Michael's school, our mouths open in wonder. The spirit of dance had taken over Michael and his classmates. No one danced better or with more passion in the whole show that night and with Michael leading the way—the JOY OF DANCE was at work. (We went into overtime, but so what!)

—Jacques D'Amboise
Author of *Teaching the Magic of Dance*, winner of an
Academy Award for *He Makes Me Feel Like Dancin'*,
and Founder of the National Dance Institute

The Renaissance

At one time, everyone danced naturally, learning steps and rules from observation and participation; dance was impulsive, instinctive, and free—a spontaneous response to rhythm, an expression of religion, even a means of working off masculine energy (for example, the German *schutzplattler*, Greek *pyrrhic*[1] and *gymnopaidiai*[2]). Dance was a manly, peaceful substitute for war, the primary profession of nobles, and was considered a manly art—an equal to horsemanship and fencing. As social and ritual lives became distinct, dancing lost its connection to war, harvest, fertility, and religion; and people danced for community and entertainment. Dramatic changes occurred with the advent of the dancing master (dance teacher), and with teaching as a profession came the beginning of dance theory and dance manuals. Though many of the first dancing masters in the mid-fifteenth century were Jewish (William the Jew of Pesaro being one of note), northern Italy and France led the way in the development of dance professionals, a vocabulary of steps, and the codifying of dances.

The sixteenth century was a time of elegance, splendor, and grandeur of lifestyle for nobles of England and France, countries in which the court fostered the concepts of grace and beauty. Dance was a basic

DEFINING POPULAR DANCE

The term *popular dance* has many interpretations. For the purposes of this book, it refers not so much to common people, or folk, as opposed to aristocrats, but to trends and developments in dancing, which were mostly in the courts during the Renaissance and early Baroque periods and in dance halls and ballrooms in later periods. Certainly, commoners were dancing, perhaps more in the rustic style than in the noble and courtly style of royalty wherein both dancing masters and peasants were borrowing steps from each other. However, by the mid-1700s, the most popular dances were done by all—"high" society and the middle and lower classes. Trends, new steps, and new dances were often the invention of ordinary people.

By 1800 in both Europe and America, popular dance was enjoyed on two levels—watching dance in theaters for enjoyment and dancing at balls and parties for enjoyment. Social dances made a circuit from the village to the court to middle class drawing rooms to the dancehall. Dances seen in theaters were copied by the general public, and popular dances were stylized by performers, appearing in revues and theatrical productions. In the twentieth and twenty-first centuries, we might describe popular dance as any dance that people enjoy doing or watching. People *do* ballroom dancing in social situations, and they *watch* theatrical productions, movies, and television programs in which choreographed dances are performed with a high degree of skill. More than in any other time period, there is a continuous crossover between theatrical performance and dancing for pleasure.

social skill; the nobility and upper class had dance lessons from childhood—every day. Because dance was the main form of social interaction, being a good dancer was a necessity. Dance was a part of good manners, and a person was expected to know how to dance in order to be accepted at court. Sequences had to be practiced exactly, because there was no room for improvisation. The coordination of hands, wrists, and arms in counter rhythm to the feet took exacting and rigid schooling.

Social dancing was not a product of nobility; rather, it had a more common or humble origin, with dancing masters adapting folk dances to aristocrats. Although folk dances and those done in the courts shared steps and influenced each other, their purpose and styles were different—folk dances were unrestrained and exuberant compared with the restraint and correctness, mathematical precision, and design of court dancing. Even clothing influenced the way people danced. Courtly dress restricted how and what could be done. Men wore tight clothing and pointed shoes that protruded up to two feet from the toes; ladies' dresses had long trains (as much as five yards of heavy material), metal or bone sewn into corsets that prevented bending, and the considerable weight of jewelry worn to impress suitors. Some ensembles weighed as much as 150 pounds. Courtiers dressed elaborately with cloth of silk and gold, real jewels, and heavy brocades, satins, velvet, and lace. Because small mincing steps were necessary and because arm and shoulder movements were restricted, dances relied on elaborate geometric floor patterns. The originality, emotion, and spontaneity of the masses became fixed forms proscribed by dancing masters. Impulse, enjoyment, and passion yielded to rules of aesthetics, exact **figures**, steps, and positions. Early social dance, once filled with originality, became the artificial product of dancing masters.

EARLY DANCES

The English **measure** was a slow, ceremonious choral dance full of changes. Shakespeare called it "mannerly, modest, full of state and ancientry."[3] The **branle**, called *brando* by Italians and *brawl* or *round* by the English, refers to a balancing motion with the chainlike joining of hands and sideward movement of dancing couples in open file or closed circle. A choral round dance of inexhaustible variations in the Middle Ages, it was scorned as a *public* dance in Italian society in the sixteenth century but embraced and refined by the French court and given a prominent

A group of men perform the morris dance in Yorkshire, England, during modern times. Originating during the Middle Ages, the dance is based on manly strength and vigorous arm swinging.

place in balls as a series of three branles to begin the evening—a sedate form for older people, a livelier one for younger married couples, and the rapid branle gai (gay) for young dancers.

The **morris dance**, most closely related to the life of British people, was popular in the Middle Ages, revived in 1899, and is still found today. Originating in ancient Celtic rituals, fertility ceremonies, community well-being, and planting festivals, it was also connected to Scottish sword dancing. A leaping dance based on manly strength and vigorous arm swinging, morris dancing was done in the streets as well as in churches. Six dancers hung with bells and carrying sticks, one with a hobby horse around his hips and one in female disguise, danced forward, back, in a circle, and in a chain, meeting and interweaving in a succession of figures. A combination of Moorish and Spanish dancing, the morris (Moresque) appeared frequently in the sixteenth century in villages and as a court dance or **masque**. Eventually, sets and props were added to make morris dances into ballets.

Shakespeare refers to morris dancing in *All's Well That Ends Well* (II ii.21) in which he makes it clear that the morris dance was commonly performed on May Day (May 1).

In the early seventeenth century, the *Book of Sports* by King James I lists amusements that may be enjoyed on Sunday, including "May games, Whitsun ales and morris dances, and the setting up of May-poles. . . ."[4] Some suggest that morris dancing comes from the Spanish Moors, others speculate that its origin can be traced to the fourteenth-century "Fool's Dance," for which dancers dressed as the court jester. Because the dances had pagan origins and were performed as part of ancient fertility rites, they had magical powers intended to attract good luck, whereas the music, bells, fluttering handkerchiefs, and clashing sticks were the means to scare away evil or malevolent spirits.

The **saltarello** was a light, fast, jumping dance enjoyed by commoners, although only the best dancers would leap and jump; it included gesture (acting) and pantomime. A favorite in the fifteenth century along with **basse danses** at court, it became a dignified, grand, restrained dance compressed into a rigid procession. By the end of the fifteenth century, pantomime left social dance entirely, although its popularity flourished in the court ballet. Couple dances were simple, stately, and grave, although youth, then as now, sought livelier, more exciting versions.

Germany, like England, had few social dances, but its close turning dances were very popular. In the **landler**, also done in Austria (Bavaria), couples danced face-to-face with both hands on the partners' backs. Often done at weddings, the dance consisted of the lady turning rapidly under the man's hand or couples skipping with hands overhead, passing back-to-back, and spinning in a close embrace. From the fifteenth century, church sermons spoke against the impropriety of turning dances with their kissing and embracing, because they were thought to be obvious love pantomimes. The shameless kissing (bussing) of women and maidens was considered uncouth, although in Shakespeare's England, kissing while dancing was considered good manners, and the lady expected it.

DANCES OF THE LATE RENAISSANCE

In 1565, Catherine de Médicis brought French provincials to court to entertain the nobles with lively folk dances during a feast at Bayonne, an early "performance." As a patron of dance, Catherine sponsored the creation of the *Ballet Comique de la Reine* in 1581 to celebrate the marriage of her sister and the brother of Henry II. Although ballets were known earlier in Italy, the *Ballet Comique de la Reine* is believed to be the first to combine music, dance (mostly geometric patterns), acting, and procession in a single theme, thereby becoming the first modern integrated theatrical dance drama.

A formal processional basse dance, the proud and showy **pavane** allowed men at court to strut about with pomp and stateliness, known as "peacocking oneself." The dignified use of cape and sword suggested the spread of a peacock's tail. This dance was an appropriate method to find a husband or wife—men could demonstrate their dancing skills, and women could show their comeliness and a large portion of their father's fortune in jewelry and fine clothing. With the addition of the *fleuret*, in which the feet flick (or thrust), the pavane lost some of its serious and pompous nature. Brought to England in 1501 by Katherine of Aragon, the pavane was commonly done at court, but never by peasants, who were more likely to dance folk dances such as **hornpipes**, **jigs** (**gigues**), flings, and **reels**. Some of these folk dances became popular at court as amusing diversions.

The **galliard** was the regular dance performed as a suite after the pavane. It was a bold, lively dance of courtship and coyness consisting of leg thrusts, leaps, swift turns, gliding steps, and foot stamping. It was the only dance performed bareheaded with hat in hand. With shouts and cries, spectators encouraged the girls to execute light-footed leaps and stamps and lightning-swift turns. An outstanding galliard dancer needed to have energy, agility, a clear brain, and quick reflexes. Anyone who did only the *cinq pas*[5] was considered a clod. In 1602, Cesare Negri wrote in his dance manual *Le Grazie d'Amore* five rules of etiquette and described 50 galliard variations, including the *salti del fiocco*, in which the man spins while leaping to kick a tassel.

It was common knowledge that Queen Elizabeth I danced a half dozen galliards as her morning "workout" before breaking her fast. Being a fine dancer herself, Elizabeth demanded the highest dancing skills

CATHERINE DE MÉDICIS

An amazing woman who broke from tradition and made an immense impact on the society of her time and upon history in general, Catherine de Médicis (1519–1589) was an Italian who became Queen of France. Born to the Medici family of Florence in 1519, she was betrothed in 1534 to Henry of Orleans who took the French throne in 1547 as Henry II. Short in height and wanting to make a grand impression for the wedding ceremonies, Catherine consulted a Florentine cobbler who provided her with the first version of the modern high-heeled shoe, which caused a sensation at court. After Henry's death in 1559, her young sons Francis II (briefly), Charles IX, and Henry III succeeded him, allowing Catherine to become queen regent.

Considered one of the greatest queens of France, Catherine is credited as the person who started ballet. Through her love for dancing, she brought Italian dance masters to the royal court and threw grand spectacles. In 1581, Catherine hosted the first ballet spectacle, *Ballet Comique de la Reine*, for the Duc de Joyeux's marriage. Balthazar de Beaujoyeulx (also known as Baldassarino Belgiojoso), who later became the Valet De Chambre (dance master), created the ballet, its design providing the essential ingredients and form of future ballets. Catherine's interest in architecture led to the construction of the Tuilleries Gardens and the new wing of the Louvre Museum. She was a great patron of the arts and helped the Renaissance flourish.

The galliard was a lively courtship dance that consisted of leg thrusts, leaps, swift turns, gliding steps, and foot stamping. The dance is depicted in this late sixteenth-century woodcut from the book *Orchesographie* by Thoinot Arbeau.

from the men and women in her court. Under her watchful eye, gentlemen jumped higher and turned more vigorously to show off for the ladies, and maids who failed to please her majesty might be chastised in public. The galliard was the great athletic dance of the Elizabethan period; gentlemen danced galliards because the physicality of the tournament and jousting had disappeared and sport was not yet in vogue. Dancing master Thoinot Arbeau considered dancing to be the peaceful counterpart of war, equal in exercise to fencing. And, he said, you could attract the ladies at the same time! However, the age of the galliard was short because the dance deteriorated into an athletic display that was considered a vulgar form of showing off.

Another imported courtship dance, the **canary,** came to France by way of Spain from the Canary Islands in the mid-sixteenth century. Spanish explorers described the dancers as hopping on one leg similar to a bird hopping on its perch. Consisting of wild, exotic skips, leaps, and turns combined with heel and sole stamping, it was considered extremely difficult, performed only by those with great skill because it was improvised with dancers choreographing their own variations emphasizing vigor and athleticism. It is believed to be the ancestor of the Spanish **jota.**

Considered the mother of the waltz, the volta originated in Germany but quickly made its way to France by 1556. A popular court dance, the volta is depicted in this seventeenth-century painting of Marguerite de Valois, who was queen of France from 1589 to 1599.

The **volta**, considered the mother of the waltz, originated in Germany and was introduced to the French court in 1556 by way of Italy; it then traveled to England. Couples danced in close embrace facing each other (rather than alongside each other), turning constantly while leaping high into the air. It was a powerful, energetic, and vigorous dance in which partners had to move as one person. German moralists of the time called it shameful and indecent because of the way the lady was held with one hand under her busk (the flat front of her corset) and the other hand on her back in order to assist in lifting her. Equally offensive, the man's thigh was used as support under her thighs to lift and whirl her around; in addition, the dance caused the dresses to swirl and a leg or ankle to show. Arbeau was less disturbed by the "vulgarity" than

EQUESTRIAN BALLETS

Equestrian ballets came in vogue during the sixteenth and seventeenth centuries. Noblemen rode together directing their steeds to execute precise turns, leaps, and other difficult maneuvers. These displays combined music and horsemanship to showcase the balletlike quality of dressage and the coordination and precision required of light cavalry in battle. Each skillful rider on a well-schooled, perfectly trained horse had to maintain the rhythm of the gaits and the position of his mount in relationship to the other horses over irregular ground. Talented nobles could demonstrate their abilities and bravery and acquire skills needed for soldiering. This ritualized form of military display was highly valued during the reign of Louis XIII, for whom an equestrian ballet, *Carrousel du Roi*, was choreographed in 1612 for his marriage. The choreographer was Antoine de Pluvinel, director of a military academy for young noblemen and considered the father of modern dressage. The spectacle, in which riders demonstrated the fancy footwork, flashy dress, and music of the French court, was a dance combining dressage and military pomp. This demonstration of chivalry and horsemanship took place in the Place Royale (now Place des Vosges) in Paris, where a large pavilion for the guests was erected. When the carrousel drew before the king and queen, the mounted chorus of nobles performed a succession of geometric figures, pirouettes, and kicks to the amazement of the royal party. The ballet had to be repeated the next day by popular demand.

by the possibility of dancers becoming dizzy; besides, Arbeau argued, ladies knew how to protect themselves with girdles and pantalets especially designed for that purpose.

By the end of the sixteenth century, the **sarabande** had arrived in Europe from Central America and had become a popular (though often vilified) dance, favored especially by the Spanish. Though the melody had a noble, haughty air, it was a wild, sexually suggestive dance done by couples. In Spain, zealots of the day considered it so repulsive and indecent that men caught doing it were given 200 lashes plus six years in the galleys (ships), and women were banished. However, by 1599, it was danced regularly in Barcelona and, by 1618, at Spanish Court. In 1623, the lines in a Spanish comedy called it old and outmoded, although it did not reach the French court until 1625. It was completely out of fashion by 1697.

Although dance at court in England was somewhat accidental before and throughout her father's reign (Henry VIII), while Elizabeth I was on the throne, dance, especially of amateurs, became more popular. Any excuse was used to dance, and the English continued their love of dancing for pleasure well beyond the Renaissance. Toward the end of Elizabeth's reign, country dances had been introduced to court where "as many as will" danced in a **longways**[6] set with lines of courtiers facing their partners, each couple progressing up or down the line while dancing with other couples. John Playford, an important figure in social dancing, published *The English Dancing Master Or Plaine and Easie Rules for the Dancing of Country Dances, with the Tune to Each Dance* (1651), an anthology of 104 dances; it was a repository of popular social dances that included traditional tunes and favorite music of the day. Its 17 editions, published during the next 78 years, added to the repertoire—the last edition contained 918 dances, of which 904 were longways. His book is still used today by those who enjoy doing English country dancing.

Other dances performed by nobles included the **triumph**—a balance of verse, music, and dance that became the standard manner of welcoming visiting dignitaries—and **horse ballets**, outdoor equestrian extravaganzas involving dozens of horses doing complicated geometric figures. Dance made its way into theater as interludes danced in classical comedies or tragedies, preludes or epilogues to operas, and **masques**—dramatic performances of verse about mythical creatures and Greek gods and goddesses that fused song, dance, poetry, and drama. The great British architect Inigo Jones was famous for inventing lavish sets and props for masques created by playwright and poet Ben Jonson. William Shakespeare included the fantastic themes of masques in many of his plays, such as *A Midsummer Night's Dream*, *The Tempest*, *Romeo and Juliet*, and *Much Ado about Nothing*.

> They bid us to their English dancing-schools,
> And teach lavoltas high and swift corantos;
> Saying our grace is only in our heels,
> And that we are most lofty runaways.
> (William Shakespeare, *Henry V*, Act III, Scene 5, Lines 32–35)

In 1588, Arbeau wrote *Orchésographie*, a manual that described dances and steps of the time in great detail and began the classification of dance forms. The book also provided instruction in social ballroom behavior and the interaction of dancers and musicians. It lined up dance steps next to the music, an early form of dance notation. Though originally a conversation on the nature of dancing, dance rhythms, and dance steps for the ballroom, it later became the basis for ballet posture and movement in the seventeenth and eighteenth centuries.

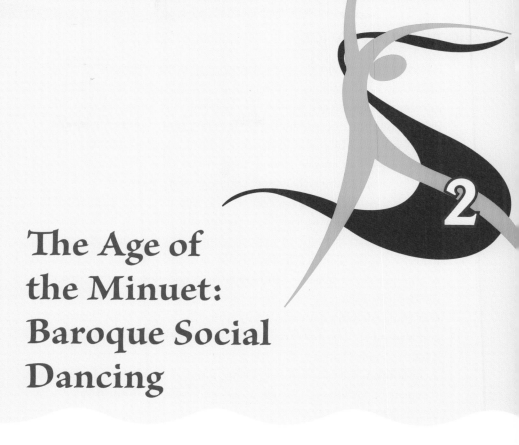

The Age of the Minuet: Baroque Social Dancing

In the mid-1600s, dance demonstrated the way of life of the French court, and this French ideal spread throughout Europe. In the court of Louis XIV, the king set the example of perfection of technique; nobility copied him, and the gentry followed. Royalty, including Louis XIV himself, often participated in ballets and operas as well as in social dancing. It was an age of splendor that admired refined elegance, opulent ornamentation, and exquisite harmony. Dancing masters were employed to give lessons in manners, social courtesies, refined education, and deportment, including the handling of hat, glove, fan, sword, and cape. A close connection existed between music and the dances of the **Baroque** period. The formal, rhythmic, melodic, and harmonic aspects of this music came alive through the formal movements and geometrical patterns of the more than 200 Baroque dances. The body was held upright with rigid torso, and space was maintained between the man and lady.

Each dance began with a bow (*réverénce*)—an essential courtesy of honoring the "presence" (king and queen) and then one's partner. The bow was formal and intricate. Dancing masters wrote chapters about it; J.M. de Chavanne devoted nearly an entire book to the subject. Only one couple danced at a time, beginning with the king dancing with the queen, then the queen dancing with the highest-ranking man in attendance, followed by the king dancing with the highest-ranking woman, and so on—each couple having a chance to show off while the rest of nobility watched the style, grace, and form of each couple.

Raoul Auger Feuillet, a French choreographer, developed a dance notation system for writing down steps and patterns, which provides us with an encyclopedia of historic dances; the first dances were published in 1700. Feuillet included illustrations showing the positions of the feet, floor patterns, and steps with no reference to arms, head, or torso; however, he was concerned with describing the figures, because anyone who danced already knew the basics. John Weaver, who translated Feuillet's work into English, wrote *Anatomy and Mechanical Lectures upon Dancing*, in 1721; it was the first book to base dance instruction on body knowledge. Other popular texts of the time were P. Rameau's *Le Maitre a Danser* (1725) and Kellom Tomlinson's *The Art of Dancing* (1735).

The **minuet** (menuet) was adopted by the French in 1670 and remained popular for 120 years. A stylized, ritual mating process and a way to honor women on the ballroom floor, the dance balanced polite distance between partners with sophisticated courtship. The minuet was a dance of elegance and noble simplicity; it was quiet, dignified, charming, restrained, and aloof. It contained ceremonial bows, dainty small steps and glides forward, back, and sideward. Partners danced side by side and separated to form loops and geometric pathways—originally a figure eight, then an *S*, a two, and eventually a *Z*. The minuet was so stylized and refined that its relationship to courtship was nearly disguised. Voltaire described minuet dancers as ones "who, most elegantly adorned, bow a few times, mince daintily across the room exhibiting all their charms, move without progressing a single step, and end up on the very spot whence they started."[7]

Although originally a dance of the people, the minuet became the darling of the court of Louis XIV. Combined with the *branle*, **courante**, and **gavotte**, it was part of a formal dance suite for which the nobles formed columns. The king and his partner performed the first dance,

A social dance for couples, the minuet became popular in France in the 1670s. The dance, which was noted for its elegance and noble simplicity, is depicted in this seventeenth-century painting by Flemish artist Hieronymus Janssens.

finishing by going to the end of the line. Each couple in turn did the same until the king was again at the front, whereupon he withdrew to the throne and left the nobles to continue dancing. By the eighteenth century, the minuet was the primary dance of instruction and nearly the only dance done at court. It was danced as an aesthetic art, performed only by the most skilled dancers. Little writing about the minuet is found in dance manuals after the mid-eighteenth century; it was considered passé by 1800, although it was still taught into the nineteenth century.

The **allemande** was popular at the court of Louis XIV and in Paris dance halls in the mid-1700s. Its chief characteristic was holding hands in many variations. It consisted of a *chassé* (sliding step to the side) and intricate versions of turning the lady under the arm of the gentleman and the man gliding under his or her arm, partners passing back-to-back, and the performance of intertwined positions such as the Italian window and the rosette. A lovely, pleasant dance, its foot movements were repetitive, the figures complicated, the carriage upright, and the arms interlaced gracefully. Before the allemande, touching was rare between partners. The many handholds and intertwined positions of the allemande began a dance revolution; the dance became a bridge between aloof decorum and more continuous touching—dancing apart as compared with close partner dancing, such as in the **waltz** of the next century.

The ***bourreé*** was a fast, light, and gay dance done in double file with a line of men facing a line of women, and the dancers moving forward and back and changing places in open style without touching. Frequently, bagpipes accompanied the dance. Although danced at a court festival in 1565 to honor Catherine de Médicis, it was primarily a folk dance. The *bourreé* was a popular courting dance, called ***rigaudon***[8] in southern France and danced only by couples. The man clapped, snapped his fingers, moved vigorously, and turned the lady by her hand while she moved more quietly with eyes downcast, while retreating and approaching.

The courante of the late 1500s was a processional dance of steps to right and left, skipping to and fro in a zigzag pattern. The rapid tempo (they are called "swift corantos" in Shakespeare's *Henry V*) was slowed considerably in France as couples marched deliberately around the hall. A favorite of Louis XIV and considered by dancing masters as basic to instruction, it was rarely danced after 1700.

The gavotte, similar to the rigaudon, had a gay, hopping quality. Traced to mountain peasants, gavottes were performed to amuse royalty by dancers costumed in the dress of the provinces from which the dances came. In the court of Louis XIV, it was danced in a decorous manner but began as a branle intermingled with galliard steps done in a circle. A four-step dance with crossing, bowing, and kissing, one couple at a time stepped to the center, where each lady and man kissed the opposite sex around the circle. At the end, the host's partner gave a bouquet to the person who was to arrange the next ball.

The gigue borrowed its name from the English jig, a courtly dance during Elizabeth I's reign. A couple dance and a form of social communication, it was introduced to the continent in the time of Louis XIV and was considered very chic in his court. It was characterized by stamping and rapid footwork, small leaps, hops, and kicks—"hot and hasty" as Shakespeare wrote in *Much Ado about Nothing*. Described in Playford's *Dancing Master*, gigues continued to be fashionable into the 1800s.

LOUIS XIV

One of the most remarkable monarchs in history, Louis XIV (1638–1715) reigned for 72 years (from age five) and ruled for 54 of those years, stabilizing France and making it one of the strongest powers in Europe. The royal palace at Versailles was an example of refined, elegant living. Louis loved dancing and wished to shine in it; he took daily lessons from dancing master **Pierre Beauchamps** for 20 years and appeared in court ballets as early as 1647, performing for 23 years. He was not the first or the only king to dance in ballets, but he was the fussi-

est and likely the fanciest. At the age of 47, Louis appeared as a nymph in a ballet. He often danced women's roles,[9] performing opposite dancer/composer Jean Baptiste Lully. In his most famous role, Louis appeared as Apollo in 1653 in *Ballet de la Nuit*, after which he became known as "the Sun King." Associated with French culture and art at its most glorious, Louis reigned over one of the greatest periods in French history as a king, a dancer, and a patron of the arts. His reign marked a peak in artistic development of ballet, and he paved the way for the transition of dance from a social recreation to a professional art.

King Louis XIV played a large role in making ballet an important part of French culture. When he was 15, Louis performed a number of characters in *Le Ballet de la Nuit* (*Ballet of the Night*), including Apollo, which is depicted in this seventeenth-century painting.

CONTRE/CONTRA/ENGLISH COUNTRY DANCING

By the end of the seventeenth century, the old branle had been transformed into an English **contredanse**, or country dance, with a variety of figures. Accepted everywhere by nobility and gentry alike, the variety of geometric designs and movement of lines was entertaining for both the participants and the spectators. At weddings, balls, and banquets, and at court, only minuets and contredanses were danced. Large leaping steps disappeared from social dancing as steps became small and graceful. The contredanse was to be danced by all who enjoyed rhythm; it was a pastime without serious purpose. While instruction in the minuet was detailed and formal, sometimes requiring books of more than 1,200 pages that described every movement and nuance of the dance, descriptions of contre merely listed a few lines of basic positions and matter-of-fact directions for movements. The dignified and formal steps of the minuet gave way to the pleasure, informality, and charm of the longways. Country dances involved figures of arches, stars, changing places, circling, crossing over, falling back, swinging partners, **hey**, and other patterns. Instead of one couple at a time dancing while facing the presence, many couples faced each other across the set; partners danced with each other, with the next couple, and so on as they progressed to the end of the line. The dances allowed everyone to meet and dance smooth interweaving patterns in harmonious cooperation.

The popularity of contredanse for commoners meant less emphasis on the culture of the nobility. Dancing masters felt that social order, standards of behavior, and the rules for balls had taken the enjoyment out of dancing, that a party should not be a course in etiquette. Although initially the French dancing masters opposed the informality of the contre, the English dances were popular throughout Europe by the late seventeenth century. The impersonal character of the dances made it easier for classes to mix; even servants could be called upon to complete a set because everyone was doing the same dances. Their truly sociable nature allowed each couple to meet and dance with every other couple during the course of one dance. These dances, which are in Jane Austen's book *Pride and Prejudice*, with their weavings up and down the set were perfect matches for the architecture of English homes and their Chippendale furniture. Once public balls (assemblies) became the fashion, the longways was the primary form of dance, although minuets still opened balls.

THE FRENCH COTILION

While the English and American colonists danced the minuet and **English country dances**, their forms were changed in France. The English danced in long rooms or public assemblies, but the French danced in the salon, which was square. French dancing masters adopted the English round for eight, naming it *contredanse Francaise* or *French Cotilion* (Anglicized as **cotillion**). Danced by four couples facing in a square formation, the dance consisted of 10 to 12 changes—advancing and retreating, circling, changing partners, and winding through each other in a grand chain—alternated with a standard figure. Several figures were linked by "changes," the most popular being the **promenade**. The first and third couples usually danced the figures, repeated by the second and fourth couples. Complicated figures danced by the top (head) two couples and repeated by the sides were alternated with chorus figures.

THE FRENCH QUADRILLE

The **quadrille** de contredanse was a dance for 4, 6, 8, or 12 dancers, originally performed in elaborate French ballets in the eighteenth century. Their popularity brought them into the French salon, where they became a dance for four couples using music that had five movements in different time signatures. Popular in Paris during the rule of Napoleon, the quadrille was brought to England in 1815 and arrived in America within a year. In America, it was danced to opera, popular tunes, and even master works. Because steps and figures of early quadrilles were complicated, dancers were given printed directions before a ball.

A seventeenth-century revolution in the arts brought both ballet and opera from the ballroom to the stage and began the clear distinction between artists and audience, creators and spectators. What had been exclusive to court went to public theaters; dance spectacles formerly for aristocrats only were now available to paying audiences. With the

During the eighteenth century, the quadrille became popular in France and quickly gained favor in the royal court. Eventually, by the early nineteenth century, it was introduced to England. Here, the quadrille is performed at the Court of St. James, or British royal court.

opening of the Académie Royale de Musique et Danse in 1661, greater artistic demands, and elevated artistic standards, the light diversions of amateurs became serious work for professionals. Amateurs could not compete in the "noble" style with those who were seriously studying the art. During the reign of Louis XIV, technical perfection was paramount, leading to artistic strength that required clarity and balance (though not necessarily vitality, naturalism, or expression).

The court choreographer and musician Jean-Baptiste Lully was appointed royal composer of music before he was 20. As a dancer and musician, he insisted on composing entertainments with scenes linked by a coherent plot, thus devising the music drama. Lully became interested in theater when he collaborated with Moliere to produce the *Comedie Ballet*. A dancer and a playwright, Moliere had a taste for the acrobatic and often included dance interludes in his plays. He was responsible for masking the characters Pierrot and Harlequin, borrowed from the ***Commedia D'ell Arte***.[10] In his play *The Bourgeois Gentleman* (*Il Bourgeoise Gentilhomme*), a triumph of comedy ballet, he wrote:

> There is nothing so necessary for men as dancing . . . Without dancing a man can do nothing . . . All the disasters of mankind, all the fatal misfortunes that histories are so full of, the blunders of politicians, the miscarriages of great commanders, all this comes from want of skill in dancing. (I, 2)

With the establishment of the Royal Academy, Louis XIV engaged many musicians, poets, and painters; women were finally allowed to dance the roles of women, and audiences moved from completely surrounding the dance floor to three sides and then to the front. Although no women appeared in public theatrical dances in France until 1681, they did occasionally dance in court performances before invited audiences. Courtiers and ladies still enjoyed dancing for pleasure, but performance became the job of the professional. Nobles and country folk gave up the pretensions of courtly dance and enjoyed cotillions and English country dancing, using the minuet as the ritual first dance.

The foundations of classical ballet began with its proscribed positions and movements, dividing popular (social) dance and theatrical dancing into two distinct forms. The French Revolution in 1790 delivered the final blow to the courtly style and aristocratic manners.

English poet Soame Jenyns demanded equal rights for dance with the other arts:

> Hence with her sister arts, shall dancing claim
> An equal right to universal fame;
> And Isaac's Rigadoon shall live as long
> As Raphael's painting, or as Virgil's song.

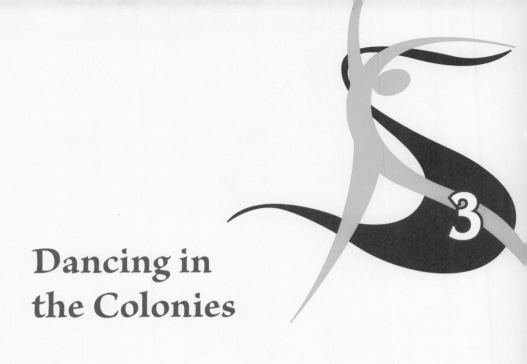

Dancing in
the Colonies

Along with other traditions from "the old country," dancing came to America with the colonists. The early dancing masters introduced the newest popular dances from Europe along with variations developed in the biggest cities, such as Boston and Philadelphia. By 1685, at least two dancing masters traveled from town to town in America, teaching figures and steps to adults and children in cities and on plantations. George Washington paid a dancing master to teach his stepchildren and his nephews and no doubt picked up some of his dancing skills there, as well as at the homes of his neighbors and brothers.

Balls and assemblies were held in governors' mansions, inns, and the most fashionable homes, even in Puritan New England, where ordination balls were the norm for welcoming a new pastor. Colonial society danced minuets, Irish jigs, reels, and cotillions, the night ending in the wee hours with English country dancing. As balls—or routs, as they were sometimes called—often began in the early evening, a night of dancing could be quite long. At some assemblies, rules were specified that no card playing could occur until the minuets were danced. Regulations at a 1790 ball in Richmond, Virginia, limited minuets to four and fancy dancing to a half hour so that less formal dancing could be done in which young and old could dance together.[11] In the eighteenth century, dances allowed men and women to mingle publicly in social settings, to form friendships, to assist romance, to demonstrate genteel manners, and to relate economically and politically. Gentility and skill at dancing were marks of success and badges of civility. These signs of proper behavior were on public view on the dance floor. Although diaries offer the most detailed information about dance in the pre-Revolutionary period, newspaper reports of social events appeared occasionally; for example, an article concerning a post-wedding party at the home of Nathaniel Shaw in Norwich, Connecticut, on June 12, 1769, reports that 92 guests danced 92 jigs, 52 contradanses, 45 minuets, and 17 hornpipes.[12]

Not everyone in the colonies favored dancing. Although some Puritans in New England enjoyed occasional dances in their communities, others were dead set against them; and clergymen were divided on the issue of dancing, particularly when it occurred on the Sabbath. William Prynne wrote in his 1,000-page book *Histrio-Mastix* that all good Christians should abandon dancing: "Dancing serves no necessary use. . . . The way to Heaven is too steepe, too narrow for men to dance in . . . No way is large or smooth enough for capering Roisters, for skipping, jumping, dancing Dames but that broad, beaten pleasant road that leads to Hell."[13]

Dancing masters, however, cared little about the Puritan values and continued to promote the fashions, dances, and sophistication of European society. Skillful dancing masters were in demand both in big cities and in rural areas because not knowing how to dance showed a lack of good breeding. It was common for dancing masters to carry a *pouchette*—a small pocket-sized fiddle used to accompany their pupils—as well as a small book of dance tunes and a manual of dance technique. The alliance between the colonists and the French during the Revolutionary War brought dancing masters, who opened schools throughout the new nation and introduced the quadrille, the forerunner of American square dancing.

COTILLION/QUADRILLE

The cotillion came to the colonies from Europe around 1770 and became a favorite dance at assemblies, as the figures allowed dancers to change partners as well as to demonstrate their expertise. Complex steps and the invention of new dances undoubtedly kept dancing masters employed. Popular in America until 1820, dancing masters reworked and improvised figures, thereby extending their usefulness and giving themselves jobs. In 1788, John Griffith published the first dance book in America—*A Collection of the Newest and Most Fashionable Country Dances and Cotillions, the Great Part by Mr. John Griffith, Dancing Master, in Providence*—which contained 13 cotillions, 9 of which had French names (for example, *La Beaute* and *La Petite Provice*). Eventually, the term *cotillion* meant fancy dress ball, and the dance itself merged with the quadrille. In the nineteenth century, the cotillion became a dance competition or took the form of dancing games for couples to meet, greet, and change partners with hundreds of variations of figures using the waltz, **polka,** or **mazurka** steps. In the twentieth century, the term was used to describe a formal dance, dance party, or dance group/club.

After the War of 1812, Americans refused to do English dances, and "French squares" or quadrilles became popular replacements, forming the basis of American square dancing. Reduced to two couples, each set of quadrilles danced patterns independently of the other sets, sometimes joining other couples in a hey to end the dance. More decorous than **contras**, the formal deportment of the quadrille had its effect on women's fashion. By 1825, the chemise gown was replaced by wider skirts and multiple petticoats. Crinoline was used to stiffen the skirt, and ladies affected a new "delicacy." In the 1820s, the figures (instructions) for many dances were called, often by a fiddler.

FORMING A MORE PERFECT UNION

Despite hardships during the Revolutionary War, balls were a way of escaping for a brief period and attempting a semblance of normalcy. Although the Continental Congress passed a resolution in 1774 prohibiting public balls, it did not succeed in ending them, even in Philadelphia; and private balls continued during the war. Not only were generals

Washington and Rochambeau skilled dancers, but they also believed that dancing helped maintain morale and provided exercise, especially in winter camps. Rochambeau, in fact, built a ballroom pavilion at his headquarters in Newport, Rhode Island, and sponsored many dance parties. While the militia encamped for the winters during the Revolutionary War in Valley Forge, Pennsylvania, and Morristown, New Jersey, officers and soldiers alike enjoyed dancing to pass the time with fife, fiddle, flute, or just whistling to provide accompaniment. At Valley Forge, the hospital staff hired a dancing master to teach every afternoon. In 1782, Captain Erasmus, in winter quarters on the Hudson River, wrote in a letter to his friend Alexander King, "We have built ourselves a large ballroom in which we are instructing ourselves in the polite arts of Dancing and fencing."[14]

With the arrival of French reinforcements in 1778, numerous balls served to show the French that Americans were indeed cultured and could step elegant minuets. Although modest homes, taverns, and camps were a far cry from the elegance of London or Paris, it was not unusual

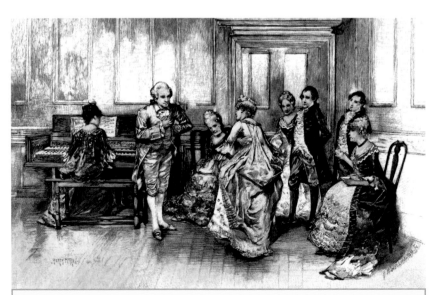

During the Revolutionary War, both the British and the Americans used dance as a form of recreation during their free time. George Washington, depicted here dancing a minuet at the home of Sally Fairfax in colonial Virginia, was especially noted for his dance skills.

GEORGE WASHINGTON

Beyond his tall stature and splendid figure, George Washington (1732–1799) was known as a man of natural grace and elegance of air and manners. He was considered an accomplished dancer and one who could, and did, dance the night away. In a 1776 letter, Gaston de Maussion wrote, "the General is exceedingly fond of dancing and never misses an opportunity to indulge . . . sometimes when he is alone with Mistress Washington at his country house of Mount Vernon, he dances with her . . . and delights in it."[15] The minuet, which was in fashion during the Revolutionary War, especially displayed his skills, and he was known to dance jigs, reels, and contras long into the night. One of his favorite dancing partners was Kitty Greene, wife of General Nathaniel Greene. In 1780, at a dance hosted by the Greenes, General Washington bet Kitty that he could win a stamina contest, and they both danced for three hours without sitting down.[16] At his birth-night ball in 1795, Washington toasted the dancers at the Philadelphia Dancing Assembly to "long continue in the enjoyment of an amusement so innocent and agreeable."[17] Martha Washington's grandson wrote that following the general's performance of a minuet, French officers commented that his dancing "could not have been improved by a Parisian education."[18] By 1775, Washington was expected to open every assembly he attended; as he traveled through the country during his presidency, festivities routinely included balls at which the local ladies could dance with him. Between his years as commander of the army and terms as president, more than 40 dances were written in his honor, entitled Washington's Minuet and Gavotte, Washington Assembly, George Washington's Favorite Cotillion, Washington and Liberty, Mount Vernon's Fancy Dance, and others (many of which are done today).

for French officers to be entertained by the citizens of towns through which they marched. Troops of Rochambeau and Lafayette were invited to parties and balls, often given in their honor. Social events helped to provide relaxation during the planning of the Yorktown campaign, where the dances entitled A Successful Campaign and The Dance (to the tune of "Yankee Doodle") started the ball. These assemblies brought together military leaders, influential politicians, and foreign diplomats, and functioned similarly to embassy parties and military officers' clubs later in history.

More than one dancing master came to the colonies from Europe. It was not unusual for them to be performers as well, bringing to the stage the very dances they were teaching; therefore, some of the theatricality of the stage was infused in the social dances. For example, on July 2, 1782, *The Maryland Journal* announced that Frenchman Louis Roussell would teach twice a week in Baltimore-Town the "Minuet, Jigg, Reel, Matelotte, Allemande, the French, English, and Dutch steps, in short every Dance requested by those who shall honour him with their company, at his school." On a third day, he would teach English country dances and the cotillion. Roussell's name appears in Baltimore theater playbills from 1782 to 1786, and the famous John Durang credited Roussell with teaching him the "correct stile of dancing a hornpipe in the French stile, an allemande, and steps for a country dance."[19]

JIGS, HORNPIPES, AND REELS

When the Great Potato Famine (1845–1852) left thousands of Irish people starving, a huge immigration brought their jigs, reels, and clog dances to America. With head, torso, and arms held rigid, the Irish dancer beat a fast rhythm with his feet. African slaves were introduced to these rhythms as Irish tinkers traveled around the country; slaves changed the Irish rhythm to the syncopated African beat and added loose swinging arms and body. The restrained but fast footwork of Irish dancing eventually became the **buck and wing** of American tap dancing.

Jigs were danced by all classes—professionals and sailors—in locations ranging from taverns to weddings to opera stages. Often done by a couple, jigs involved patterns of chasing, danced to African-American music in 6/8 time with onlookers cutting out the women or the couple after awhile. In 1774, Nicholas Cresswell wrote of his experience at a Twelfth-night Ball in Alexandria, Virginia: "A couple gets up and begins to dance a Jigs . . . others comes [sic] and cuts them out, and these dances last as long as the Fiddler can play. This is sociable, but I think it looks more like a Bacchanalian dance than one in a polite assembly."[20] Because hornpipes and rigadoons (done as longways) required fancy stepping, only the most skilled performed them.

John Durang, considered the first American professional dancer, adapted the hornpipe to the stage in the late 1700s. He and his family dominated the theater in Baltimore from 1810 to 1821 and taught social dancing as well. Choreographer and dancer Alexander Placide, who was trained in classical ballet and known as first dancer to the king of France, came to America in 1791 and danced the hornpipe on the tightrope. Hornpipes and jigs were popular entertainments in theaters and appeared in many forms during the first decades of the 1800s.

During the nineteenth and twentieth centuries, the Virginia reel became one of the most popular dances in the United States. Here, Confederate soldiers are depicted dancing the Virginia reel with their partners at a ball in Huntsville, Alabama, during the Civil War.

Reels were popular line dances brought by Scottish immigrants. The dances involved intricate footwork alternated with an interweaving hey, a pattern that resembled a figure eight. Three or more dancers in a straight line or in two facing lines (longways) danced with each other. Though myth would have us believe the **Virginia reel** was George Washington's favorite, danced at the end of eighteenth-century balls, there is no evidence in sources from the period that he or anyone else danced it, nor that there was a set "final" dance for assemblies. However, figures from Playford's longways dance, **Sir Roger de Coverly**, later became known as the Virginia reel.

The "shot heard round the world" in 1775 at Concord, Massachusetts, started a revolution, a change in sensibilities, and a recognition that dancing was for everyone, not just for the elite. Fifteen years later, the French Revolution brought an end to the aristocratic French court with its proscribed manners and court dancing. Many French dancing masters, in fear of losing their heads, immigrated to America. From that point on, social dancing became an activity for the bourgeois in France, the commoner in England, and "everyman" (and woman) in America.

Dance in the Western United States

4

Kentucky, Tennessee, and the North Carolina mountains remained apart from the sophisticated influences of French dancing masters in eastern cities, though Irish and Scottish settlers contributed to dance forms. Scottish reels, danced in lines or circles, were easily added to the colonial repertory, and dancing masters simplified the formal figures and steps of the minuet to create group dances. Mountain folk preferred big circle dances and square formations, later called the **Kentucky running set**. Another trademark of southern dancing was **clogging**—loud, rhythmic footwork that was a combination of Irish **step dancing**, dances of black plantation slaves, and Cherokee stamping. Considered distasteful and vulgar in New England to leap about or stamp one's feet instead of gliding lightly, clogging separated good from not-so-good dancers in southern mountain regions.

As America's frontier pushed westward, dance was a popular form of social interaction. The same dance might be done at an officers' ball with music provided by a regimental band, in a plantation home with local musicians, or in a tavern with a local fiddler or the innkeeper playing the tune. Although the figures and tunes might be the same, the "look" of the dancing varied according to the participants, the spectators, the purpose of the gathering, and the type and amount of beverages being consumed. English country dances were especially suited to dancers of varying skill; they were easy to learn, allowed dancers to interact with one another, and could be embellished to suit the ability of the performer or the occasion. By 1810, there were more than 2,800 English country dances recorded in manuscripts or other printed documents. As settlements moved west, the cotillion and quadrille went with them, becoming the basis for American square dancing. Native American women were invited to complete sets when there was a shortage of female settlers. Dance imported to America adjusted to a new environment by becoming faster, longer, and more spread out, often with shouting and plenty of energy. Only in dance competitions (the hoedown) were there solos, and if you missed a step, you were out. Instructions were given by a **caller** who cued the dancers as to what figure(s) to do during the dance and provided spice by injecting commentary on the manners of the community. Meanwhile, back east, society followed the decorum of the European drawing room and modified English country dancing.

As American settlers pushed west during the early nineteenth century, they often brought their dances with them to the frontier. In this woodcut, a couple is depicted dancing at a Kentucky wedding, circa 1800.

Without a noble class, merchants and plantation owners were the "upper crust" in colonial America, and they attempted to emulate the fashion and manners of the English.

From the time of the founding of the Mormon Church in 1830, Mormons enjoyed dancing as a part of community life and culture. Although the Mormon membership came from areas where churches were often hostile to dancing, their philosophy diverged because Mormons believed that physical welfare strengthened spiritual welfare. Dance was a socializing force as well as a means of promoting health, invigorating the body, and adding to the grace and dignity of man.[21] Joseph Smith, founder and first president of the Mormon Church, enjoyed music, drama, and dancing. At the Legislative Festival in 1852, Brigham Young, second president of the Mormon Church, said he danced so his body could keep pace with his mind to "get strength and be renewed and quickened, and enlivened, and animated. . . ."[22] Dancing in Utah was a favorite pastime. When the Social Hall was dedicated in Salt Lake City on January 1, 1853, the ceremonies ended with a grand ball. A dancing school was opened in 1853 in Brigham City. Dances were conservative, stately, and genteel. In 1870, the design of a park included a dancing bowery with a wooden floor large enough to accommodate fiddlers and three quadrille sets. Immigrants who were converted to the Mormon religion brought their own customs and dances to settlements.

Dancing was a common amusement on the frontier. Although house warmings and barn raisings varied, every new building was an occasion for dancing, drinking, and feasting, though practitioners of some religions, such as Methodists, enjoyed games and food but discouraged dancing and liquor. Dances were the universal amusement on holidays (and any other time an excuse could be found) and were held in houses, stores, barns, courthouses, hotels, amusement halls, and cabins, or on the prairie. Rounds, squares, reels (now called folk dances), and waltzes were the social dances of the day. Although they did not require a high degree of skill, they brought people together in group interaction and socialization. Foreign transplants had access to the community through dancing even when their language skills were limited. People practiced decorum and good manners at parties, balls, and cotillions.

5
The Nineteenth Century through the Victorian Era

For centuries in polite society, dancing was formal with specific measured stepping in the proper order. Though there were many versions of, for example, the gavotte, sarabande, and allemande, there was only one minuet. It was a formal ceremony, a ritual, performed exactly alike by each couple in its turn, steeped in convention and rules. The baroque technique was calm, dignified, classical, and regal. The nineteenth century brought about a romantic revolt and a new way of dancing. Even the formal minuet was transformed into a group dance done in lines or circles. Although peasants often danced with their arms around their partners' waists, in cultured society, dancing in such close proximity was considered scandalous. Where once the pleasure of dancing was partly the "show" for the spectators, dancers now turned away from the onlookers toward their partners to dance in each others' arms, whirling around the floor with other couples equally self-absorbed. Dance had truly become an integral part of society. As George E. Wilson wrote in his treatise on ballroom dancing, "In all

civilized communities, dancing is considered one of the necessary accomplishments of life."[23]

Dancing in the nineteenth century was romantic, athletic, and exciting. Highly organized balls were generally held in private homes or
rented halls. The waltz, **galop**, mazurka, and polka were inventive and
varied, allowing for improvisation, turning, creativity, and greater closeness of couples; however, the steps and patterns were planned. Dancing
masters traveled around to teach the latest and most fashionable dances,
educating youth in grace, manners, and skill and providing a valuable
form of exercise. Dances were often done to the popular music of the
day, including tunes by Stephen Foster ("Oh Susannah," for example),
Camille Saint-Saens (mazurka), John Phillip Sousa (military **two-step**
and **cakewalks**), and Johann Strauss (known as "The Waltz King"). Author Thomas Wilson, in his 1808 book, *An Analysis of Country Dancing*,
praised dance: "Dancing is the most enchanting of all human amusements, it is the parent of joy, and the soul and support of cheerfulness; it
banishes grief, cheers the evening hours . . . and brings with it a mixture
of delightful sensations which enrapture the senses."[24]

THE REGENCY PERIOD

The French Revolution caused the end of the old noble regime, court
dancing, and the aristocratic style. These gave way to social dancing as
an activity for the general public. The first two decades of the 1800s were
an era of the empire fashion—a short-waisted dress hanging straight
from under the bust to look narrow, modeled on Josephine Bonaparte's
couture. A number of dance manuals listed directions for dozens of
dances, tips for setting figures to a tune, and guidelines to proper etiquette. Guests were expected to take turns choosing and calling or leading a dance. Readers were reminded not to dance with the same partner
more than twice, and more than one dancing master commented on the
poor standard of the day and the number of dancers who lacked proficiency in steps and figures.

English country dance continued its popularity into the nineteenth
century, incorporating figures of allemande, back-to-back (later called

Another popular dance during the early nineteenth century was the galop, which was often accompanied by the music of Johann Strauss. Like the waltz, mazurka, and polka, the galop was a couple's dance that emphasized improvisation.

do-si-do in the Western square dance), and turning or swinging a partner or corner (a simple hand turn). The popular dance called tight pig included hand-clapping with opposites and partners (like the childhood game patty-cake). Dancing became even more socially accepted because Americans believed that they were just as cultivated as Europeans. Although Scottish reels might be featured, the centerpiece of the ball for middle- to-upper class Americans was the longways triple minor. The easy simplicity of the steps and unaffected graceful body made country dancing accessible to all and was an important part of courting. Author Jane Austen wrote in *Pride and Prejudice* that "to be fond of dancing was a certain step toward falling in love."

As dance schools flourished, so did the number of dancing masters and manuals. *Contredanse* became a fashionable word in society. Daniel Webster wrote that all the world was a contredanse. In the latter part of the century as other dances were introduced from Europe, contras were deemed unfashionable; however, New Englanders adopted and adapted them, adding innovations from Scottish and Irish settlers, such as the stomping **balance and swing** and the side-by-side wheel (previously courtesy turn in the English country dance). Two innovations that served to distinguish contras from country dance were the buzz step swing borrowed from French Canadians and the alternating of couples in the line from the proper set (all women on one side facing the men) to every other couple switching sides to form an improper set.

The **grand march**, or **polonaise**, replaced the minuet to open a ball elegantly and allowed all present to examine their prospective dance partners, processing around the ballroom to a popular piece of music in a circle, line, or serpentine figure.

The popular new dance of 1815 was the quadrille, a combination of French contredanse and cotillion figures. Quadrilles, requiring just two couples, used geometric patterns done in a square formation. Figures included forward and back, going to the right and left (later called siding), crossing over, **setting** to partner, ladies' chain, and promenade. Hundreds of combinations were possible, and a favorite dance throughout the nineteenth century was lancers quadrille. The French-inspired footwork was challenging; however, dancers were instructed not to kick or caper about, but rather to dance quietly and to keep the torso still, moving only from the hips downward. Many balls, whether for high society or an informal gathering, were made up almost entirely of quadrilles. Even Lewis Carroll described a lobster quadrille in *Alice in Wonderland* (1865).

See how eagerly the lobsters and the turtles all advance!
They are waiting on the shingle—will you come and join the dance?

The waltz in 3/4 time became popular in the early 1800s; it was the first dance to conquer the world without the sanction of the courts and dancing masters. With its roots in the Renaissance volta and the Baroque allemande, the hypnotic rhythm of the waltz became a new dance form reflecting new standards, although it had its critics. Peasants had danced with their arms around each other's waists for centuries, but the closed, facing position and tight hold of the waltz was considered scandalous, indecent, immodest, and obscene by the English (who had by this time forgotten how much they enjoyed the volta). Early American moralists called it disgusting, indelicate, immoral, and lascivious—a dance of loose character. In 1816, the *London Times* warned parents against exposing their daughters to "so fatal a contagion" and speculated that the waltz was probably introduced to British society by "some worthless and ignorant French dancing master."

As the waltz gained popularity, in spite of its detractors, the attitude of dancing masters was "if you can't beat them, join them." They began publishing descriptions of steps or incorporating waltz rhythms into country dances. Composers, particularly the Strauss family, helped popularize waltz music for band and orchestra. Some writers even viewed the waltz as less harmful than cotillions and country dancing. Its control and elegance copied the manners of the Edwardian era. The haste of a more industrialized age was reflected in its spirit, character, and rapid turning. Originally, the dance had the couple moving sideways and turning clockwise to keep the lady from stepping on her long gown. As hems shortened, the man was able to step forward and the lady backward to allow for both clockwise and counterclockwise turns, diagonal steps, and light kicks and leaps. Modifications and refinements led to a variety of steps—the skaters' waltz, the redova, the military waltz, the polka dot waltz, the aeroplane (to imitate an airplane leaving the ground), and even the hesitation waltz for the older couples. Known as the dance of love for its romance and passion, the waltz dominated dance programs by 1900 and was unrivaled as the social dance of choice.

The waltz was such an overwhelming success that we continued to waltz into the twentieth century, and we still waltz in ballrooms today.

Pierre-Auguste Renoir's 1883 oil painting *A Dance in the Country* shows a couple dancing the waltz. The smiling woman is a working-class seamstress named Aline Charigot, who later became Renoir's wife.

Africans took the formal waltz and created the closely clutched two-step, the cakewalk, the **Charleston**, the **black bottom**, the Lindy (or the **Lindy hop**), **rock 'n' roll**, and the **twist**. Full of invention and rhythm, these rough dances lacked the courtesy of the earlier formal courting dances, but they reflected the situation of a depressed, enslaved people. Many of the twentieth-century popular dances were invented by or inspired by African Americans, and they seemed to create something new every 10 years or so. By contrast, it took Europeans 250 years to turn the volta into the waltz.

The galop, popular in the early 1800s, involved a playful gliding or fencing step (*chassé* and hop in a one-half turn). High-spirited and demanding, galops usually followed quadrilles on dance programs. Variations of the galop, such as the wave galop, Polish galop, and the Puritan provided a lively display. A simple music style primarily for dancing in the 1840s, galop tunes evolved into bravura showpieces for bands.

The mazurka came to America with Polish immigrants. This wild, exuberant dance was tamed into respectable turns and variations. Mazurka was challenging, gallant, and graceful with a strong accented beat. Embellishments and improvisation allowed the dancers to express independence, pride, and freedom from restraint. The basic step, *pas de basque*, repeated three times was usually followed by an *assemblé*—not the ballet *assemblé*—but a connecting step consisting of a small jump with the toes together and heels apart, followed by a snap to first position (heels together, toes apart). Other variations included the mazurka hop and *pas battu*, in which men, especially, could show off their virtuosity; *pas boiteux*; *tour boiteux*; Gitana waltz; and *tour sur place*. Mazurka steps were also popular additions to quadrilles. Although the mazurka fell from favor in the late 1800s, possibly because of its technical and athletic nature, some of its steps were incorporated into the polka (polka mazurka).

THE ROMANTIC ERA

The period from 1840 to 1860 ushered in excitement, romance, and gracious dancing. Fashions were elegant; dances were natural, inventive, and fresh. By the middle of the century, the waltz had become fully accepted, perhaps in part because notable society figures were fond of it and because the galop, and later the polka, added a playful nature. The good-clean-fun quality of polka made turning in closed position acceptable and introduced thousands to the pleasures of dancing in another's arms.

Polka, the national dance of Czechoslovakia (Bohemia), became popular in the 1840s. A fast-turning dance in 2/4 time, the polka combined the waltz and galop: three steps with a hop on the fourth step. It was a joyful, spritely dance with many variations, although it was much subdued by the end of the century by reducing the three quick steps to a glide and the hop to a rise. Variations of polka steps included the two-step, *la esmerelda*, Bohemian (heel, toe), Portland, Berlin, polka militaire, ruchter, and the most popular, baby polka, in which couples faced each other for a patty-cake hand-clapping sequence followed by a walk around themselves. Imported from Eastern Europe along with the national dances of Poland (mazurka) and Hungary (**czárdás**), the polka was the most lasting in popularity.

The **schottische**, originating in Germany, became popular in England, Scotland, and America and was a favorite with youth, although it had its critics. The Highland schottische, a combination of schottische and reel, spread to America and Australia from Scotland. At the turn of the century, the two-step was born out of the schottische, most often danced to Sousa's "Washington Post March."

MID-CENTURY: THE WAR BETWEEN THE STATES

In the 1860s, attending a ball in the North or the South was one way to forget briefly the perils of war. Couple dancing was done in the open, side-by-side position in circles, in squares, or in lines while interacting with other couples. Invitation-only balls were limited to family and friends and might take place in a private home. Public balls could be attended by anyone who bought a ticket. A means of raising money for a worthy cause, during the Civil War they were used to support the war effort. A dance would likely include a grand march, Lancers quadrille, galops, schottische, and soldier's joy, often closing with the Spanish dance or Spanish waltz, set dances done in a circle or a line using waltz steps. It was improper to dance with the same partner all evening, as participants at a ball had an obligation to mingle to ensure that everyone had a pleasant time in order to forget the war for a few hours. Balls were a socially acceptable method of meeting a potential husband or wife. A gentleman might ask a lady for her dance card, choosing to ask her for a dance in which he was particularly proficient in order to impress her. A lady never refused a dance unless she felt ill or fatigued. Master-servant balls, an old European tradition, were occasionally held. At these events, servants, tenants, and local townspeople mingled; landowners might invite their most talented dancing slaves to the "big house" to perform for guests or even to compete against one another. One slave described a fellow slave as "the jigginest fellow ever was. . . . He could put de glass of water on his head and make his feet go like trip-hammers and sound like a snaredrum."[25] Still considered improper by some, **round dances** such as the waltz and polka were talked about more than danced. More than one article appeared in newspapers objecting to any kind of "frivolous" activity, such as dancing, while soldiers were dying on battlefields. Dancing, however, did have relevance to the military, as young men who would become soldiers learned through dance instruction their right from left, how to march in time and maneuver in formation, as well as the importance of cooperation and teamwork.

After the Civil War, freed slaves took clogging and jigging into minstrel shows, dancing the buck and wing (a cross between the **pigeon wing** and **buck dancing**) to make money as professionals. Southern whites and blacks continued to clog dance in rural America, while "cultured" people in urban areas adopted new dances. By the late 1800s, the couple dances were called as round dances, and there were published descriptions of more than 150 variations.

THE LATE VICTORIAN ERA

The reign of the British queen Victoria (1837–1901) was a genteel and graceful period that emphasized romance, the arts, imagination, culture, and proper etiquette. Dancing was a formal event in which ladies

RULES OF ETIQUETTE

Both in ballrooms and in everyday life, cultured individuals were expected to exhibit proper manners. These rules of etiquette—called rules of civility in George Washington's day—included the following:

- A lady always walks or dances with the gentleman on her left side.
- When walking, the lady rests her left hand on the gentleman's right arm.
- A gentleman always escorts his partner to and from the dance floor, giving her his right hand and placing his left hand behind his back.
- On a down stairway, a gentleman walks in front of the lady in order to break her fall and to avoid stepping on her gown.
- Mingling with others and dancing with them is encouraged; it is expected that one dance with as many different people as possible during the evening.
- It is considered ill mannered for a lady to turn down a gentleman asking for a dance because her rejection would embarrass the host and the gentleman.
- Couples never touch hands without wearing gloves. The gloves look elegant and dashing and keep from soiling the lady's dress with the oil from his hands.
- Dancers must always follow the directions of the dance master even if the dance is performed in a different manner from the way they were taught.
- A lady or a gentleman never asks a "stranger" to dance; rather he or she must ask a mutual friend to inquire discretely whether the intended partner is agreeable to a dance.

and gentlemen were expected to conduct themselves with propriety, and numerous etiquette books were published to provide instruction.

Young boys and girls were taught proper behavior as well as dancing, and it was common for children, especially girls, to attend finishing (or polishing) schools to learn the finer points of etiquette. It was considered improper, distasteful, and ungentlemanly or unladylike to ignore socially acceptable behavior. The Victorian ballroom was a place of beauty, formality, and grace.

In 1885, Allen Dodworth, founder of the New York Philharmonic Society, published a book about ballroom dancing: *Dancing and Its Relation to Education and Social Life with a New Method of Instruction Including a Complete Guide to the Cotillion (German) with 250 Figures.* The Dodworth Family Academy of Dancing was fashionable and famous, fighting for **ballroom dance** as a medium of education, gentle living, good manners, and cultivated behavior—a requirement for acceptance

During the late nineteenth century, ballroom dance became extremely popular in the United States and was intricately woven into the social fabric of the country. Here, the popularity of ballroom dance is evident in this woodcut illustration of President Benjamin Harrison's inaugural ball in 1889.

into society and a necessary accomplishment of life. So many manuals on social etiquette were in publication by the late 1800s that dancing masters felt their jobs were in jeopardy, fearing people might just purchase a book and then take to the ballroom. In *The Illustrated Manners Book*, the author writes, "The notion is very generally entertained that dancing can be picked up by attending balls, and the figures from observation—a most absurd conclusion."[26]

By the end of the 1800s, ballroom dancing and contact between men and women had become formal, stiff, reserved, and even ritualistic. With women attending college, entering the workforce, seeking the vote, and fighting for reform (contraception, temperance, and health care) and gentlemen frequenting their clubs and avoiding dancing schools, a greater isolation grew between the sexes. Men were often ill prepared to dance, particularly if they were to be humiliated by attempting dances of which they had little knowledge or skill, although women were still taking dancing lessons and organizing balls and parties.

Made in America

As American explorers moved west, dancing went with them. Figures and steps were borrowed and modified as America took on its melting pot characteristics. Scottish dances, particularly reels and strathspeys, were popular in the second half of the 1800s. Possibly because Queen Victoria enjoyed dancing them, they were considered chic in ballrooms and were also danced for home recreation. English county dancing became unfashionable for a while, although Cecil Sharp saved the form from obscurity by writing down the figures in the early 1900s; but other forms were emerging or combining to keep America dancing.

SQUARE DANCING

As exploration moved southward and westward, so did the population and their dances. Hardworking pioneers, in search of recreation, activity, and social contact with neighbors, looked to a reinvention of the French cotillion and quadrille, which became increasingly Americanized after the 1849 Gold Rush brought more settlers to the West. Called **square dancing** by the 1860s, the form had simple requirements—a

CECIL SHARP

Cecil Sharp (1859–1924) was a British music teacher whose interest in traditional English dance began in 1899, when he saw a group of morris dancers. Morris dancing was nearly extinct; Sharp's writings about morris dancing kept it alive. He published his *Morris Books*, starting in 1907. Between 1911 and 1913, he published a three-volume work, *The Sword Dances of Northern England*, which included the obscure rapper **sword dance** of Northumbria and long sword dance of Yorkshire. Largely responsible for reviving interest in folk dance in England, Sharp founded the English Folk Dance Society in 1911 to promote traditional dances in workshops held throughout the country. In 1932, the group merged with the Folk Song Society to form the English Folk Dance and Song Society (EFDSS). From 1916 to 1918, Sharp traveled through remote areas of Virginia, Kentucky, Tennessee, and North Carolina recording folk songs and dances of southern Appalachia.

wooden floor, music, and a caller, and either a barn, someone's living room, the town hall, or, in later years, the grange hall. These "ingredients" made it easy for pioneers to bring their dances with them. Dancing reflected the color, custom, and casual nature of life in the Wild West. Patterns challenged the dancers' attentiveness but allowed everyone to participate, even those unfamiliar with a dance, through the use of a caller, an American innovation. The caller kept order on the dance floor and allowed everyone to join the dance without having previous instruction and memorizing figures with patterns as complex as those of the quadrille.

When a caller was not around, settlers did dances they could remember, or someone in the group called the figures using a repertoire of colorful sayings and patter interspersed with the cues. Usually a rhyme in couplet form, the calls not only gave directions or commands but also referred to western life.

> Rope a yearling, brand a calf
> Meet your honey with a once and a half.

Thanks largely to automaker Henry Ford, the square dance enjoyed a revival in the 1930s and quickly spread throughout the United States. In fact, 19 states recognize the square dance as their official state dance. Here, young couples gather for a square dance at the local YMCA in Wilmington, Delaware, in 1947.

It was easy to find someone who could play a guitar, a fiddle, or an accordion to provide accompaniment. Americans and recent European immigrants brought their disparate dance styles to square dancing, creating a new form. While figures and calls varied from east to west, many of them kept their French names, such as promenade (take a walk) and do-si-do (from the phrase *dos a dos*—back-to-back). In the early 1930s, autoengineer Henry Ford became interested in the revival of square dancing as part of his New England restoration project. His efforts and the publication of his book *Good Morning* (1941) interested other individuals who adapted square dancing to contemporary America while retaining its primary flavor. Square dance groups formed around the country and can be found throughout the United States—from the Atlantic to Pacific.

FOLK DANCING

The melting pot called *America* has a rich history of folk dancing—Scottish, Swedish, Jewish, Polish, Irish, Bulgarian, Greek, and German. Finding a group of like-minded individuals who love to spend an evening or a weekend doing a form of world social dancing is easy. The location could be a college campus, a local recreation center, a coffeehouse, or a camp. Remnants of African and European dance have infiltrated ballroom dancing; those who enjoy the recreation, challenge, and social camaraderie of their heritage or who simply like to have fun have embraced the specific forms from various countries. Often called international folk dancing to differentiate it from American square dance, folk dances based on lifestyles, climate, religion, courtship, weddings, and funerals developed. Folk styles involved vigorous movement and stamping in colder areas, whereas steps were slower and more fluid in hot, humid climates. Suitable for all age groups, folk dancing has become a popular family activity, a way to foster international understanding and national identity, and a means of disseminating folklore.

Coming from the people, folk dance is transmitted from one generation to the next. Square and folk dance festivals are plentiful in the twenty-first century as are daily, weekly, or monthly dance clubs. International folk dance troupes, such as the Tambouritzans and the

Brigham Young University International Folk Troupe, and professional national companies, such as Russia's Moiseyev Dance Company and the Ukrainian State Dance Ensemble, travel around the world
performing dances in native costumes, showing the crossover from
recreation to theater.

CONTRAS

In the late twentieth century and in the twenty-first century, the tradition of New England contra dancing (simply called contra) and English country dancing has been revived. Most cities have regular weekly
or monthly dances, and fans are willing to drive many miles to seek
out their favorite dances and/or callers and musicians. As with the
English longways, couples dance in two lines of indefinite length, usually "improper" formation (men and women alternating along a line
facing their partners). The odd-numbered couples are called *actives*;
the even numbers are called *inactives*. Actives generally start the figures, dancing with or between the inactives and progressing toward
the bottom of the set while the inactives are moving toward the top of
the set, becoming actives when they reach the top. A dance may last 10
to 15 minutes as couples dance along the line. Family-friendly contra
dance events are open to everyone, regardless of experience, but many
dances offer instructions to beginners before the actual dance. A typical evening of contra dance is several hours long, interspersed with
other dances, such as waltzes, polkas, and Swedish **hambos**. A caller
instructs dancers in a walk-through before each dance begins and calls
the figures while it is in progress, typically four to six figures repeated
with each neighbor couple. Usually, musicians—rather than recorded
music—play traditional jigs and reels from Ireland, Scotland, Canada,
or America. The contra tradition in North America is to change partners for every dance. Because individuals interact with their partners
and everyone else in the set, cooperation is vital. Some enduring places to study both folk music and dance include the Buffalo Gap Camp
in Maryland, the Pinewoods in New York, the Stockton Folk Dance
Camp in California, the Maine Folk Dance Camp, and the Augusta
Heritage Center in Elkins, West Virginia.

COUNTRY AND WESTERN DANCE

Country and western dance emerged as dance steps from the polka, the waltz, and other folk dances were combined with traditional square dance figures and couples broke away from the square. With the invention of the radio, country and western music spread through the nation after World War II, and the dance form grew in popularity, especially in bars and **honky-tonk** dance clubs. Its popularity hit mainstream America after the film *Urban Cowboy* with John Travolta was released. Suddenly everyone was wearing cowboy boots and Stetson hats. Country and western dances use pre-set steps to specific songs or tempos, such as **cotton-eyed Joe**. A primary two-step pattern with variations of handholds such as the double-arms-over move similar to movements necessary to tie up a calf,

After the movie *Urban Cowboy* was released in 1980, country and western dancing grew in popularity throughout the United States. Here, couples participate in country and western dance in Fort Worth, Texas.

might comprise an entire dance. The form lives on in line dancing, which was popularized in the 1990s and done in clubs and as aerobic exercise. Dancers perform a sequence of steps, usually about four to six, in lines all facing the same direction and make a quarter turn at the end of each sequence before repeating the patterns. With the release of the hit song "Achy Breaky Heart" by Billy Ray Cyrus in 1993, a phenomenal rise in the popularity of country/western music and dance occurred.

NATIVE AMERICAN DANCES

From the Atlantic Ocean to the Pacific Ocean, Native American Indians have always danced. Dancing was social, religious, and ceremonial, occurring at festivals as entertainment or ritual; special days were set aside exclusively for ceremonies and dancing. Dance contributed to culture by teaching social values, training for war, acquiring skill and grace, contributing to recreational life, and entertaining and honoring the gods. Because society and religion were bound together, ceremonials were foremost in the life of Native Americans, and dance was a necessary part of ceremonies and social festivities. Rituals and dances were a means to maintain harmony between humans and the supernatural world and to give thanks to or request aid from spirits and gods, to honor visitors, and to express friendship. Social dances concluded festivities and provided an opportunity for diversion, fun, and socializing. Often, dances had animal and bird names (dove, rabbit, and raccoon) and lasted not more than 10 minutes. Everyone—from children to the elderly—was invited to participate. To call dancing popular would be a vast understatement. Dancing was interwoven throughout the whole texture of Native American customs and society. Native Americans *danced* their religion, their social beliefs, and their customs. As Henry Rowe Schoolcraft wrote in 1848:

> Dancing is both an amusement and a religious observance among the American Indians, and is known to constitute one of the most wide spread traits in their manners and customs. It is thus interwoven throughout the whole texture of Indian society, so that there is scarcely an event, important or trivial, private or public, which is not connected . . . with this rite.[27]

Throughout the United States each year, Native Americans gather for powwows that educate, communicate, and demonstrate that native peoples are alive, vibrant, and dynamic. Here, Native American dancers perform at the National Powwow in Washington, D.C., in 2005.

Many dances and rituals of Native American tribes have changed very little over centuries and are still practiced today; others continue to evolve to reflect the social trends and events of the times and contact with other peoples. Tribes gather throughout the country for **powwows** that educate, communicate, and demonstrate that native peoples are alive, vibrant, and dynamic. Distinctly Native American, the powwow is a unique spiritual gathering central to the full cultural experience because it perpetuates and reinforces native culture and tradition. All ages, sexes, and people come together "shaking the earth" to honor spiritual beliefs and ancestors and to join in friendship. In his book *Powwow*, George Horse Capture (A'aninin) describes the meaning and impact of the powwow:

While vigorously dancing, an irrefutable awareness arises that I am close to the center, to the essence of life. As the world dissolves in color and music around me, a warm spiritual feeling spreads throughout the heart and body, and the song and dance carry me away from the heat and earth . . . My feet, body, and arms move automatically to the rhythm of life. My fellow dancers are part of me and I am part of them. I realize that life could not get much better than this moment and it is a gift from the creator.[28]

LOVELY HULA HANDS

In the Hawaiian Islands, dancers are keepers of the knowledge. There was no written language for nearly 2,000 years before Captain Cook arrived in 1778. Traditions, genealogies, and life stories were passed down through chants, stories, and dances. The arrival of shiploads of British and American Protestant missionaries and the colonization of the islands during the Victorian age changed Hawaiian society and culture. Many of Hawaii's indigenous dances were lost as missionaries imposed strict religious rules in their ignorance, misconceptions, and belief that Hawaiian dances were sexual. During the last 125 years, the dances have been reclaimed and honored for their traditional meaning.

There are two ancient forms of traditional Hawaiian dance: *ha'a*—a sacred movement to supplicate the gods and performed by men in outdoor temples (called *heiau*), and **hula**—varied and complex dances done for commoners outside the heiau and characterized by music, poetry, dance, and mime. Originally a means of promoting beauty, health, healing, and fertility, hula instructs, inspires, and educates. Hula is an interdisciplinary art, embracing literature, mythology, genealogy, language, protocol, botany, and craftsmanship. It provides social and historical commentary on themes such as people, gods, materials, and dances for royalty and nobility, and it is associated with values, beliefs, and practices. Using stylized movements that pantomime the text of song (called *mele*), the hula is graceful, athletic, dramatic, and uplifting, full of pelvic circles and ellipses, heel stamping, and foot twisting. The curvilinear form of hip rotations and sideward, weighted sway is very earthbound.

Movements represent life in the Hawaiian environment—volcanoes, surf, birds, and people. The hula dancer fuses the self with forces of the universe—birds, fish, wind, water, flowers, and Pele (goddess of fire and volcanoes)—to provide both dancer and audience with awareness, enjoyment, and a higher level of spiritual consciousness.

Native Hawaiian dances barely survived the Christian influence. Changes occurred after 1820, including the disappearance of temple dances and dancers; the scattering of heiaus; women dancing traditional men's dances; an increase in the absorption of European steps, clothing, and rhythms; and the introduction of string instruments (mandolin, guitar, and ukulele), which modified the music. In 1830, the hula was officially banned by Queen Ka'ahumanu, but it was reinstated in 1840. When King David Kalākaua, the "Merrie Monarch," took the throne in 1874, he wrote and supported chants, music, and dance beginning with a royal sanction of the hula as the symbol of Hawaiian identity. His reign included the first royal attempt to study and catalog the oral traditions of hula. With the forced capitulation of Queen Lili'uokalani, Hawaii was annexed to the United States in 1898; and the influx of visitors—American, French, and Japanese—caused greater modifications in the hula to appeal to tourists as an "attraction." The twentieth century changed the look of the hula and the sound of Hawaiian music as they were adopted by Hollywood and American radio; the Hollywood film *Bird of Paradise* (1932) began a nonstop love affair with Hawaii. The radio broadcast in 1935 of *Hawai'i Calls* from the Moana Hotel and Bing Crosby's huge hit "Waikiki Wedding" inspired dreams of surf, sand, and paradise across America. A cotton or grass skirt often replaced traditional tapa cloth. By the 1950s, Hollywood, radio, contests and competitions, television, exhibitions, and statehood (1959) made all things Hawaiian popular on the mainland and with tourists visiting the islands.

The Early Twentieth Century

7

At the turn of the century, the Industrial Revolution in America brought more people into cities, and new social institutions emerged—cabarets, dance halls, theaters, movies, and amusement parks. These public performance venues gave rise to greater social mobility and a massive consumer culture. The debutante ball became one method of entry into a social community. The movement, rhythm, and manner of early twentieth-century dances produced a new aesthetic for social dancing as well as a revised code of social behavior. Rather than the formalized learned patterns of earlier dances, leading became the man's role, guiding the lady around the dance floor with improvised steps and determining what changes or variations would be danced—something an eighteenth-century couple would have found extremely disorderly. Social dances moved into public areas, such as dance halls, restaurants, and hotels, with smaller dance areas and dim lights; couples danced closer together and were hardly aware of other dancers on the floor. Where nineteenth-century balls had been held in private drawing rooms or in assemblies with the utmost decorum, "modern" ballroom dances drew criticism and questions: Were these early dances indecent? Were they too wild, abandoned, irreverent? Would **ragtime** music corrupt the young? Might the dances being done in dance halls result in crime or lack of moral behavior? In 1914, Pope Pius X banned the tango for its "barbaric contortions," and newspapers and magazines ran articles questioning whether this modern form of dancing was "proper." Popular dance forms of the early 1900s directly impacted social and cultural changes.

Once called scandalous (as new dances often are), the waltz was considered tame and old-fashioned by the turn of the century. The speed of the steps had increased to produce the **Viennese waltz**, in which couples flew around the ballroom turning furiously, but only the most skilled dancers could maintain the pace. A fresh dance emerged, called the **Boston**, which was technically a waltz; however, it was slower, took twice as long to complete a turn (four measures instead of two), and included sideward movements that were less rigid and more exciting. Even with these restrictions, the dance still required a lot of space. The older turned-out foot positions disappeared from the ballroom to remain only in ballet and other stage dance forms. Partners danced hip to hip with natural foot positions. Although the Boston died out by World War I, its easy-going style and emphasis on the emotion of melody transferred to new dances such as the **foxtrot**.

THE RAGTIME ERA

In spite of the many dances devised in Europe during the Renaissance and Baroque periods, after 1850, the only new European invention was the French **can can**, a dance by women who could kick high, jump into splits, and swish their skirts; however, the can can was exclusive to dance halls and cafés because it was considered unsuitable for respectable ladies or gentlemen (but nonetheless popular to watch). Innovations in dance after 1850 came from South America, Cuba, and America. Although most dances in the nineteenth century had been imported from Europe, in the early twentieth century, Americans were bored with the old music and dances that came from their grandparents' generation and found pleasure dancing to "modern" ragtime music that came from the South. Americans sought innovation and found it in the **one-step**, **Texas Tommy**, **animal dances**, and the foxtrot, although much of

Dancers from Paris's Moulin Rouge nightclub perform the can can in 2006. Though Europe was known for the development of dances prior to 1850, the can can was the only dance of major importance that was created after that time.

the upper class rejected these dances because of their association with blacks, bars, and brothels.

The 12 million Africans brought to North and South America as slaves had traditions of dance and music that were integral parts of their culture but that were largely prohibited by white society. Typical movements such as pelvic rotations and foot stamping became mixed with country jigs and clogging, forming a unique style that white Americans found culturally threatening, forcing blacks to gather in juke joints and honky-tonks away from the public eye (whites). These run-down establishments were the incubators for new music—**blues**, ragtime, and jazz—and new dances—the buck and wing, the Charleston, the black bottom, and the grind. T.D. Rice (1808–1860), the first white man to appear in blackface and perform parodies of African American songs and dances, and William Henry Lane (1878–1949), aka "Master Juba," brought African American dance and music to the public through minstrel shows. For more than half a century, the African American's search for respectability and dignity was tied to popular dance. One of these, the cakewalk, had a life both in the minstrel show and as a social dance. Originally thought to be a way in which slaves mocked the pretensions of their masters, the dance met the public eye on the **vaudeville** stage. Couples danced around the stage (and eventually the dance floor) in imitation of their betters, leaning back, prancing, and taking elaborate steps and leaps hoping to "take the cake"—the prize to the best, most inventive dancers. By 1900, the cakewalk was so popular that the black musical *Clorindy* helped establish the habit of stage productions introducing popular dances to the public.

Where the cakewalk went, ragtime music followed. A mixture of white tunes and black drum rhythms, ragtime's syncopation appealed to a public itching for something new and exciting. Its most famous proponent, Scott Joplin, wrote the "Maple Leaf Rag" in 1897 and "The Entertainer" in 1902, tunes still popular today; Irving Berlin's "Alexander's Ragtime Band" (1911) illustrates the enduring popularity of this music as the dancing public went ragtime crazy. Soon musicians and composers realized they could fuel the public frenzy for new dances and music by including the instructions for steps in the lyrics of the songs, and dances passed from stage to dancehall and vice versa for nearly 30 years until motion pictures and Broadway made dances too complicated for the average dancer to imitate. Songwriters frequented nightclubs in search of dances that could be sold to an eager public. The formality of dances such as the waltz gave way to animal dances, including the bullfrog hop, possum trot, snake hip, eagle rock, lame duck, and **turkey trot**. For all classes these dances provided a new freedom, a reaction against the restricted movements and outdated lifestyle of the 1800s.

As usual, moralists of the day criticized animal dances because they were of African heritage; they encouraged physical contact; and some, such as the bunny hug and the grizzly bear, required dancers to hug—complaints similar to the ones about the waltz in the previous century and the volta three centuries before. Outraged by these "vulgar" dances, the Vatican denounced the turkey trot in 1914 and also the tango, for good measure. The Dancing Teachers' Association of America refused to teach ragtime dances, and a turkey trotter in New Jersey was sentenced to jail for 50 days. Clearly, dancers were pushing the boundaries of sexuality and decorum, and the survival of these dances was left to Vernon and Irene Castle who refined them and gave them subtlety, elegance, and acceptable style.

As professional entertainers, the Castles invented new dances, performed them, and taught them to ordinary people who could dance them anywhere. They invented the **Castle walk**, introduced the **maxixe** from South America, popularized the foxtrot, and cleaned up the **tango** that was invented in Argentine nightclubs. The Castles popularized the turkey trot in the Broadway show *The Sunshine Girl*. Their African-American music arranger Ford Dabney took nineteenth-century rhythms and

THE CASTLES

Vernon and Irene Castle set the world on fire between 1911 and 1918, first in Paris as exhibition dancers and then in America as performers and teachers. Moralists thought dancing face-to-face was vulgar; but the Castles' inventive and tasteful style changed Western social dancing into a form that was intimate, improvisational, and natural but easily copied by ordinary people. They were the first entertainers in more than 150 years to wear contemporary clothing while dancing rather than costumes. A slender, graceful, proficient dancer, Irene set the standard for the way American women looked, dressed, and danced. Considered the most fashionable woman of the day and much more attractive than the "pleasingly plump" look of the time, she made dieting popular. Because the speed and size of the steps required vigor and a more flexible body than a bustle or hoopskirt could allow, Irene refused to wear tight corsets, preferring light girdles, knickers, and free-floating skirts of light materials. Everyone copied her changed them into the syncopated, rapid, and spirited jazz beat, which spread over three continents.

The foxtrot (from Fox's trot) was the most popular of all because it was a relaxed, uncomplicated dance that was easy for inexperienced dancers to learn. Invented by Harry Fox for his vaudeville show finale, Fox's trot (a dancing strut) was adopted by the show's patrons for the Club Jardin de Danse above the theater. Both slow and fast versions (from 28 to 50 bars per minute) appealed to the public. Dance teachers created variations—a mix of the quicktime foxtrot and the Charleston, known as the **quickstep**, and a slow version called the saunter. Adults enrolled in dancing schools to learn to dance in the sophisticated Castle style. Descriptions of new steps appeared in magazines every month,

ravishing gowns, her petite Dutch cap (much more sensible for theatergoers than the enormous hats that blocked everyone's view), and even her bobbed hairstyle. Catering to high society, the couple opened Castle House to teach "correct dancing" and performed in their Castles in the Air cabaret. They standardized and refined the turkey trot, cakewalk, and tango and created the Castle walk, Castle house rag, Castle half and half, **Castle lame duck waltz**, the hesitation waltz, and the one-step. They were vaudeville's highest paid act, earning $5,000 a week compared with the average American salary of $10 to $15 per week, and they appeared in Irving Berlin's first musical comedy, *Watch Your Step*. Their success resulted from pioneering a new way of dancing, changing African improvisation into standardized steps, replacing suggestiveness with elegance, and emphasizing the upright torso. No more wiggling, twisting, shaking, or flouncing. Creating the cult of good taste, their success resulted from their being a wholesome, "modern," married couple who were the "proper" models for social dancing.

allowing for practice at home as a result of the invention of the phonograph and records. Couples went out to dinner in order to dance af-
terward at restaurants that hired orchestras for nightly entertainment.
Even the elite Vanderbilts hired an instructor to teach them to cakewalk.
Essentially, Americans and Europeans were dance crazy (especially ragtime crazy) before World War I. Between 1912 and 1914, more than 100
new steps fed this dance mania.

When the tango came to America via Paris, it was considered the
epitome of degradation. It was born in the brothels of South America,
where dancers acted out the ritualistic relationship of prostitute and pimp.
Quite possibly, its seedy reputation and suggestiveness contributed to its
popularity. Comprising more than 100 steps, the passionate and provoc-
ative tango dramatically used the body with mixed rhythms, quick turns,
action steps, and rests. The steps of the tango were sexual and aggressive,
and the typical music played on violin and accordion suggested longing
and despair. The dance swept Europe and America with sensation and
outrage, although the Castles tamed it into a standardized, less rebellious
version. Dancers wore evening attire and polished shoes and simplified
the steps but kept their sensual quality. Tangomania affected everything
from fashion to food. Men's evening dress became more elegant and
sleek. The gliding steps and fast sharp turns led to women's dresses with
sexy slits to allow freedom of movement, though some women prevented
intimate contact with their partners' bodies by wearing bumpers on their
dresses. Irene Castle wrote, "It was against the law to dance too close to
your partner . . . and bouncers in restaurants tapped their patrons on the
shoulder when they got closer than nine inches."[29]

The tango was responsible for the popularity of tea dances (tango teas) held at restaurants, hotels, and department stores at which
unescorted ladies could find a partner with whom to dance. These meet-
ings provided another opportunity for moralists to complain. The Savoy
Ballroom in Harlem held tango dinners where patrons could dance between the courses of a meal. Dance halls and cabarets not only hosted
dancing, but they also became a symbol of a new freedom for women—a
hotly debated idea. The evil influence of dance clubs on young ladies was
considered "a straight chute down which . . . thousands of young girls
descend to the way of the prodigal."[30] Although the tango nearly faded
after World War I, a less rebellious, more standardized version emerged

During the early 1900s, the tango became quite popular in the United States, where the dance was embraced by women and men alike. Here, actress Betty Blythe dances the tango with the head of the Park Lane Dancing School in the 1920s.

and was popularized by Rudolph Valentino in his 1921 film *The Four Horsemen of the Apocalypse*.

The maxixe, or Brazilian tango (tango Brasileño), used steps and movement from the polka and mazurka, rhythm of the Cuban **habañera**, and syncopation from African music. Using the two-step and *chassé*, it was an energetic dance characterized by swooping body motion, alternating action with rests. Steps could be done in close embrace and in skating position side by side. The maxixe had a short life before World War I but was later revived as the **samba**.

The outbreak of World War I left little time for frivolous pursuits like dancing; the maxixe and animal dances fizzled away, although the tango did not die out completely.

VAUDEVILLE

As the popularity of ragtime began to subside, its replacement—jazz—took off, especially in vaudeville. Born during the era of technological and industrialization growth and radical changes in popular entertainment, vaudeville covered a period from the 1870s to the 1930s. The building of new cities and theatres and a hunger for new acts allowed ethnic and racial minorities to break into "show biz" and to obtain a broad cultural visibility on the stages of taverns, inns, honky-tonks, riverboats, saloons, and legitimate theaters. The sources for vaudeville include the Italian commedia, traveling medicine shows, the circus, dime museums, and the English music hall. The typical vaudeville show had 10 to 15 variety acts—comedy, juggling, singing, dancing, and magic—and was the primary form of popular entertainment in Europe and America. New York City became the center of entertainment, and its performers were likely the first American stars. Vaudeville shows frequently sent their best on to Broadway and/or Hollywood, notably Mae West, Fred Astaire, Ginger Rogers, Bob Hope, Buddy Ebsen, Ray Bolger, W.C. Fields, and Enrico Caruso. An impressive spectrum of dancing in vaudeville included jigs, clogs, tango, tap, ballet, soft shoe (also known as the sand jigs), ballroom, **cooch**, schottische, **shuffle**, and modern interpretive dance. These became dance crazes and contributed to modern dance and the genre of musical theater. White vaudeville often employed young black dancers as backup (chorus) dancers. Black performers could get work, show off their talent, and gain valuable experience as "picks" (short for piccaninny, an offensive term for black children), often providing their own choreography and performing tap, soft shoe, and even Russian dancing for stars such as Sophie Tucker and Mae West. White artists were not above stealing the dances these picks created and taking credit for originating them—the **shimmy**, for example, which had been around for a century. When young picks got too old or too big, they

THE HARLEM RENAISSANCE

The **Harlem Renaissance** covers a 30-year period between 1900 and 1930 in which African-American dancers, singers, and writers were viewed favorably by white audiences who flocked to Manhattan to see new shows. Originally a Dutch settlement (Nieuw Haarlem), the area now known as Harlem became home to Irish immigrants before becoming a neighborhood for blacks and Hispanics. Audiences were introduced to stars such as Josephine Baker at the Lafayette Theatre; the **swing** sound of Dizzy Gillespie and the Lindy at the Savoy Ballroom; the Charleston at the Lincoln Theater; Duke Ellington's Orchestra; and the greatest dance acts, including the Nicholas Brothers and Bill "Bojangles" Robinson, at the Cotton Club.

performed on the black vaudeville circuit at salaries that would still be impressive today. Although a few dancers were successful on both the white and black circuits (most famous, Bill "Bojangles" Robinson, called the Chocolate Nijinksy, and Joe Frisco, billed as the world's first jazz dancer), most never broke out of the black revue.

A particularly successful show, *Darktown Follies*, opened in 1913 at the Lafayette Theater in Manhattan. It broke the taboo of showing a Negro love scene on stage and introduced the world to the Texas Tommy and the wildly popular **ballin' the Jack**—a circular serpentine, shuffling dance related to the "ring shout" done on Southern plantations in which the head, shoulders, and feet stayed still while the torso, hips, and knees swayed and undulated:

> First you put your two knees close up tight, sway them to the left and sway them to the right, step around the floor kind of nice and light . . . that's what I call ballin' the jack.

The Texas Tommy had only two basic steps—a kick and three hops on each foot followed by a choice of turning, sliding, or pulling, allowing the dancers to improvise steps and break away from each other before rejoining hands. Another feature of *Darktown Follies* was the circle dance, used to close the second act, in which the entire company snaked around the stage with their hands on the hips of the person ahead. Combining the **mooche** and a slide, the last person in line performed a version of ballin' the jack. The production ended with the cakewalk. It was such a sensation that Florenz Ziegfeld purchased the entire act for his Ziegfeld Follies.

The Roaring Twenties

Reacting to the industrialized age, greater freedom, and prohibition, Americans frequented nightclubs, speakeasies, ballrooms, and restaurants featuring large orchestras. Some of the most famous Manhattan and Harlem ballrooms include the Grand Plaza, the Tropicana, the Palladium, the Savoy, the Manhattan Casino, and the Cotton Club.

The Charleston, probably the quintessential representation of the 1920s, was done at home, at private parties, and in public in restaurants and ballrooms. Born in the African-American show *Running Wild*, its roots go back to the **Ashanti** ancestor dances of Africa. A form of challenge dancing, the Charleston made the cover of *Life* magazine in 1926 and swept through America and Europe. The Prince of Wales was considered quite accomplished at it. From its appearance in the show *Shuffle Along* in 1921, the Charleston was a sensation. (*Shuffle Along* also marked the beginning of the idea that black dancing was not as "low life" as previously thought, introduced tap dance to white audiences, and helped create the craze for jazz dance.) According to *Variety* magazine, the Charleston was responsible for the tragedy at Boston's Pickwick Club—its collapse, causing the death of 50 people, resulted from the vibrations of too many dancers. Although its popularity was rather short, the Charleston took couples away from intimacy and toward individual expression, blurred the lines between performer and ballroom dancer, and produced the idea of "cutting in" where dancers could change partners mid-dance. It also boosted the careers of many performers, notably Ginger Rogers and Joan Crawford, who began their careers as Charleston stars. Charleston steps showed up in the Lindy hop of the 1930s, in the mashed potato of the 1960s, in the quickstep, and in street dancing and stage performances of the New Kids on the Block of the 1980s. It remains an icon of the Jazz Age and of the young flappers who kicked their way through the 1920s.

The black bottom replaced the Charleston in popularity around 1926, when it was done in the show *Scandals*. Another sensation that set the public wild, its ballroom version was little more than shifting the weight from foot to foot with a few single or double stamps, a slap on the backside, a shimmy, and an occasional kick, though its ancestor, the **Jacksonville rounders' dance**, was more intricate. Accomplished dancers and creative choreographers merely repackaged it so that it was popular both onstage and off, illustrating again the closeness of the stage, the screen, and the dance hall.

The **big apple** originated in Columbia, South Carolina, at the Big Apple Night Club and swept the country when adopted by college students. Like early swing and square dancing, the dance used a caller to indicate which couple should "shine" by performing their unique version of the steps while surrounded by other dancers. Steps included the **shag**, breeze the knees, jump back jack, Charleston jump, mooch, spank the baby, London Bridge, scarecrow, the **boogie woogie**, the **Suzy Q**, and the praise Allah. Dance instructor Arthur Murray seized the opportunity to promote both a new dance and his business by giving some of the steps call names such as "peel the apple" and "cut that apple."

DANCE MARATHONS

In the 1920s, dance contests were the rage, developing from hour-long events to Depression-era entertainments that went on until the last couple was left standing. Amateur dancers sought prize money, food or gifts, and fame. The first documented marathon in America was in

An iconic figure in American dance, Arthur Murray performs for a class of teachers at one of his dance studios in 1946. Murray opened his first Arthur Murray Studio in Minneapolis, Minnesota, in 1938. By the end of the 1970s, there were more than 3,500 studios in the United States.

March 1923, when Alma Cummings wore out six partners more than 27 hours of dancing, breaking a British record. Newspapers reported on her partners, shoes, clothing, diet, and religion. Fanned by youth culture, freedom of expression, the recent women's right to vote, and the Depression, marathons represented the survival of the fittest. Entering a marathon was often an act of desperation. Skill at dancing—the best dancers taking the prize—became secondary to the ability to stay on one's feet. In some ways, dance marathons were theatrical events,

ARTHUR MURRAY

Arthur Murray (1895–1991) studied under the popular dance team of Irene and Vernon Castle and began teaching dance for them in 1912. He won his first dance contest at the Grand Central Palace, a public dance hall where he later became a part-time dance teacher. While he was a student at the Georgia Institute of Technology, he taught dance at the Georgian Terrace Hotel and organized the world's first "radio dance"—a band on campus that played for about 150 dancers atop the roof of the Capital City Club in downtown Atlanta while broadcasting on radio. His brilliant idea was to teach simple dance steps to prospective dancers with footprint diagrams placed on the floor, which they could follow to learn how to dance. It became a successful mail-order business with more than 500,000 dance courses sold within a few years. After Murray married his dance partner, Kathryn Kohnfelder, in 1925, they franchised dance lessons by training dance instructors for the Statler Hotel chain. Their business grew when Murray picked two little-known dances, the big apple and the **lambeth walk**, and turned them into dance crazes. Soon his name became a household word, synonymous with ballroom dance. He called ballroom dancing "conversation set to music." His schools guaranteed that pupils would learn to dance in 10 lessons. He popularized the **varsouvienne**, and after World War II, he capitalized on the popularity of Latin dances. From 1950 to 1960, *The Arthur Murray Party* was broadcast on primetime television. By the late 1970s, there were 3,560 Arthur Murray Studios, and there are still hundreds around the world with instructors trained in his style.

similar to today's television reality shows—compete, suffer, endure, fail, or triumph. Spectators cheered their favorites or heckled contestants they hoped would lose, creating excitement, drama, and controversy. If either partner's knees touched the floor, the couple was disqualfied. Winners represented the American dream; losers typified "real life" in America. Marathons became big business, though not necessarily ethical business. Some promoters went to small towns, opened a show, sold seats (and resold them when vacated), and then left without paying the prize money, raking in the cash but giving marathons a bad name. Dancers, promoters, and spectators produced the illusion that something important was happening in spite of the contestants' exhaustion or pain. The blood, sweat, and tears of the dancers provided a livelihood for promoters. Eventually, this "dance or die" ethic aroused criticism, and reformers protested the exploitation of women and minors. Cities and states passed laws prohibiting conducting or participating in marathon dance contests on the grounds that they were harmful and unregulated, attracted undesirables, and were scams run by con men. Although the 1920s and 1930s dance marathons vanished, they lived on in the form of the roller derbies of the 1950s, the twist contests of the 1960s, and the popularity of twenty-first-century television talent shows such as *So You Think You Can Dance* and *American Idol*.

As the popularity of jazz increased, it attracted both a growing audience and campaigns to censor the "devil's music." By 1930, at least 60 communities in the United States had enacted laws prohibiting jazz in public dance halls, blaming it for the evils of the day. Thomas Edison, inventor of the phonograph, said that jazz would sound better played backward. In places where jazz was played, speakeasies attracted customers from varying social backgrounds, and whites and blacks were allowed to mingle for the first time. The racial integration and the belief that jazz encouraged sexual activity were reasons for those critical of jazz to crusade against it; however, trumpet player Louis Armstrong and composer Duke Ellington helped propel jazz to a higher level.

LATIN RHYTHMS

While America was blending dances that originated in Africa with Irish, Scottish, and English forms, South and Central America were fusing African dancing with their own rhythms. One product was the habañera,

THE SAVOY BALLROOM

Opened in 1926 as a luxurious ballroom, the Savoy had a burnished wood dance floor (250 by 50 feet), two band-stands, a dazzling cut-glass chandelier, a soda fountain, tables, a marble staircase, and a disappearing stage at one end. It was considered Harlem's premiere dance space, and it could hold thousands who wished to dance in a refined atmosphere rather than in small, stuffy, smoke-filled night-clubs. The Savoy owners had *The Finest Ballroom in the World* inscribed on its entrance marquee. With its racially mixed clientele, older dance forms alternated with new dance fads—the waltz, the Charleston, the shag, the **slow drag**, the Lindy hop, the **shim sham shimmy**, the **tranky doo**, the **peabody**, and the **mambo**; in fact, many dances were developed there. The Savoy insisted on polite, con-siderate etiquette and the best music of the day. Its dance floor was treated with reverence—dancers were not al-lowed to smoke or drink on the floor, and it was stripped and polished every night. A variety of dance activities—Afro-Caribbean; the annual Harvest Ball; Arabian, Rus-sian, and Chinese nights; and even **barn dances**—attract-ed various communities to the Savoy, created a genteel atmosphere, and enhanced its reputation. An estimated 25 million pairs of feet danced their way across its floors seven nights a week between 1926 and 1958.

a nineteenth-century folk dance blending the French contredanse, Eng-lish country dancing, and African slave dances. Born in Cuba, the dance spread through South America and Spain and influenced other dance styles, notably the **milonga**, which combined the European polka, the Cuban habañera, and dances of the gauchos (cowboys of Argentina). By the turn of the twentieth century, economic prosperity, growth in population, and industrial expansion in Buenos Aires rivaled that of New York City. The number of bars and brothels in the port city was considerable; there young "toughs" came to drink, brag, swagger, and dance the milonga, combining steps with thoses of an African dance, the candomble, thus creating the passionate, erotic, and proud tango. Surprisingly, this dance with its seedy origin swept the world when upper-class Argentinians traveling to Europe took the tango with them to the ballrooms of Paris.

The Mid-Twentieth Century

BALLROOM DANCE MEETS BROADWAY AND HOLLYWOOD

Beginning in the 1920s, New York City was the place for dance. You were defined by what, with whom, and how well you danced. Musical comedies on Broadway reflected the taste of their audiences and taught them new dance steps, etiquette, social graces, and the conduct of romance. They also helped people escape from the harsh realities of the Depression. The trend that started during vaudeville of "selling a song" by attaching a dance to it continued on Broadway. Social dance numbers became top-selling sheet music and records, frequently with dancers' images on the cover and dance instructions included. The most popular were recorded twice—as a song and as music for dancing at home. The foxtrot was especially useful in that the choreography of steps and positions of the dancers could be varied, to show sophistication, disdain, rapture, devotion, snobbery, or competitiveness. The ballroom (couple) version of the Charleston was introduced to "society" in the *Ziegfeld Follies of 1923*. The Charleston lasted over other 1920s dances because of its versatility—it could be performed solo, in couples, or choreographed into a group dance; steps could be simplified (for social dancers) or embellished (for stage); and the movements looked great with the fashions of the day (slit, fringed dresses for women and casual jackets and slacks or tuxedos for men). The fastest way to stardom was to be cast in a movie as a flapper with a Charleston or black bottom number; African-American teacher Billy Pearce was credited with training many Broadway dancers in Charleston, black bottom, and tap dancing.

Parallel to the 1920s themes of independence and choice for women, plots in musicals often focused on the major life decision—a suitable marriage partner. Courtship was a central theme of operettas and musicals—boy meets girl, loses girl, and wins her back—which ended with the happy joining of appropriate couples. Dance scenes illustrated or resolved conflicts and complications in the plot; gave clues to character; and depicted romance, celebration, or suspense. Chorus members were young and provided a framework for featured dancers who were often popular vaudeville dance teams with singing, dancing, and comedic talents, such as Fred and Adele Astaire. Song and dance were integrated into the dialogue to further the plot and establish chronology (as in Jerome Kern's *Showboat*, which covers 1887 to 1927).

Hollywood musicals, which began when "talkies" took the place of silent films, also brought popular dancing to the public. From 1928 to 1951, studios such as MGM, Warner Brothers, and RKO produced lavish musicals (often film versions of Broadway successes) in which the dancing used social dance forms as well as tap, ballet, jazz, or eclectic combinations. Movies such as *Top Hat*, *White Christmas*, *On the Town*, *The Wizard of Oz*, and *An American in Paris* had lavish dance routines performed by stars such as Gene Kelly, Eleanor Powell, Judy Garland, Ray Bolger, Fred Astaire, and Ginger Rogers. The romantic grand waltzes and pseudo-foxtrots of Fred Astaire and Ginger Rogers sent scores of filmgoers to seek ballroom dance studios. Rogers's girl-next-door image made her a trendsetter for women throughout America, who tried to copy her style, her wardrobe, and her haircut—much as they had done with Irene Castle 30 years earlier. A precursor to the shorter music video of the 1980s and 1990s, the era of spectacular Hollywood musicals saw the borrowing of dance movements back and forth between the general public and film choreographers.

(continues on page 92)

ASTAIRE AND ROGERS

Fred Astaire (1899–1987) and Ginger Rogers (1911–1995) are still the most famous dancing couple on film. Though each had a separate career—Astaire dancing in vaudeville and on Broadway with his sister Adele, and Rogers starring in both comedy and drama on stage and screen—their magical partnership, unique chemistry, and unforgettable dance routines were unsurpassed. They presented a new kind of romance, sophisticated yet accessible, in which dance scenes took the place of gooey love-making. Paired with choreographer Hermes Pan, they created famous dance routines—each one challenging, elegant, and innovative. They worked together in 10 films from 1933 to 1949—*Flying Down to Rio* (1933), *The Gay Divorcee* (1934), *Roberta* (1934), *Top Hat* (1935), *Follow the Fleet* (1936), *Swing Time* (1936), *Shall We Dance?* (1937), *Carefree* (1938), *The Story of Vernon and Irene Castle* (1939), and *The Barkleys of Broadway* (1949). Their more than 16-minute dance— "The Continental"—in *The Gay Divorcee* is the longest dance number in movie musicals; and it was filmed in one continuous "take," including a Charleston section with chorus girls in bathing suits and heels, and Astaire and Rogers's sweeping descent of the staircase in the finale. Chorus girls were the fantasy figures of the day; they had a public image that fell somewhere between a Dallas Cowboys cheerleader and an adult performer. Astaire and Rogers helped change that image.

In all, Fred Astaire made more than 40 movies (both musicals and dramas), performed in 16 television shows, and was named "Entertainer of the Century" 30 years before the century was over! Mikhail Baryshnikov has called him the greatest dancer ever. Ginger Rogers starred in 73 films, won the 1940 Oscar for Best Actress for her dramatic role in *Kitty Foyle*, played Dolly in 1,116 performances of *Hello Dolly* on

LIFE

ASTAIRE & ROGERS DO THE YAM

AUGUST 22, 1938 10 CENTS

Though their movie careers ended decades ago, Fred Astaire and Ginger Rogers are still the most famous onscreen dance couple in Hollywood history. Here, the duo is featured on the August 22, 1938, cover of *Life* magazine doing the yam during the movie *Carefree*.

Broadway, played Las Vegas and elsewhere in her own show, and did hundreds of guest spots on television. Both received the Kennedy Center Honors for Artistic Achievement.

(continued from page 89)

LATIN DANCES

In the 1920s, African music and movement became the source for acceptable social and theatrical dance. African rhythms were brought to the Americas with slaves, and the rhythms were blended with European melodies and instruments to form new musical styles and steps with more pelvic and torso isolations than those seen in the formal European couple dances. During the Depression, dancing was a means of lifting spirits and leaving troubles behind—the gaity of swing raised morale. The music was electrifying, and the vitality of the dancing was infectious.

During World War II (1939–1945), these black rhythms were fusing with Latin music, and big bands and band leaders popularized the Latin sound in ballrooms and restaurants and on radio and television shows. Cuban-American bandleader Xavier Cugat (1900–1990) was instrumental in spreading Latin music in the United States. His resident orchestra at the Waldorf-Astoria Hotel before World War II and later on television followed the trends and made records of the **conga**, the mambo, the **cha cha**, and the twist when each was in fashion. In 1955, Pérez Prado's cha cha version of "Cherry Pink and Apple Blossom White" reached the top of the pop charts and stayed there for 10 weeks. As new generations adopted updated versions of the mambo, the **rhumba**, and the cha cha, they incorporated jazz rhythms and borrowed turns and steps from swing and foxtrot.

The first Cuban dance with African overtones that came to the United States was the slow, seductive rhumba (spelled *rumba* in America), which, in the 1930s, introduced the distinctive Cuban hip motion. In 1950, the mambo—an Afro-Cuban hybrid of swing and rhumba—brought its energy, speed, and rhythmic beat to the dance floor. In the late 1960s, the **bossa nova** had a short run of popularity; in the 1980s, the sultry **lambada** was a brief craze; and toward the end of the century, **salsa**, a faster version of mambo, became the "in" Latin dance.

Latin dance refers to conflicting practices. Its emphasis on sexy hip movements and interplay between the partners is evident in both social and competitive styles of Latin dancing, but the commercialism of cookie-cutter dance studios has all but removed the improvisational character from Latin dance. Dancers from South America and the

Caribbean think of their dances as a demonstration of cultural pride, heritage, identity, and participation in Latin "community." With a flexible spine and dynamic torso, dancers shift or suspend steps between their feet, with bent knees, and they improvise movements following the rhythm of the music. Latin dance is alive, creative, and constantly changing. The ballroom versions have specific, predetermined steps and postures performed with a straight spine and complete transfer of weight from foot to foot. The ballroom studio dancer has training, technique, polish, and discipline, whereas the Latin street dancer goes for flavor, fire, emotion, and "soul"—a natural response to one's partner and the musical rhythms. The ballroom dancer maintains a stable frame and a connection of torso, legs, and feet, whereas the street dancer uses the body to mimic the sounds and accents of the musical instruments—improvisation is a highly esteemed skill. The ballroom performance is a well-rehearsed routine to impress an audience; the street dancer may have spectators watching, but he or she has little interest in their opinion.

SWING AND THE LINDY HOP

Jazz music replaced **tin pan alley** in the late 1920s, and swing music soon led dancers to experiment with new movements. Louis Armstrong helped create this new swing sound by producing music that emphasized African rhythms played with a big band sound and by improvising solo with his group ensemble. This syncopation encouraged faster footwork and the bouncy style that characterized swing dancing. The modified Texas Tommy, two-step, and Charleston steps became known as the Lindy, or Lindy hop, named as a tribute to Charles Lindbergh's 1927 solo flight across the Atlantic. During the 1930s, steps were continually invented and added to the Lindy as dancers tried to outdo each other, and the breakaway allowed partners to improvise various steps based on vernacular dances, such as the Suzy Q, **shorty George**, gazin' the fog, scarecrow, and **truckin'**. The most accomplished dancers were found in Harlem's Savoy Ballroom. The Lindy contributed enormously to jazz dance used in theatrical productions of the late 1930s to 1950s.

During World War II, swing music and dancing helped Americans escape from the miseries of the Depression and wartime. American soldiers put an end to English stoginess by taking the **jitterbug** overseas; the departure from the sedate, closed position to sending the partner out to arms' length increased the dynamics of swing. Tunes such as

FRANKIE MANNING

Frankie Manning (1914–2009), legendary Lindy hopper, was famous for his innovative routines, introducing the air step and developing and teaching the Lindy hop. Starting at the Savoy Ballroom as a teenager, he became choreographer and dancer for Whitey's Lindy Hoppers, a group whose spectacular exhibitions in nightclubs, in ballrooms, in Broadway and Hollywood musicals, and on stages around the world helped spread and mold the dance form. His professional career slowed around 1955; but when partner dancing made its comeback in the 1980s, following the rock 'n' roll era, Frankie was coaxed into sharing his knowledge. Swing dancers began to study with the master, to commission his choreography, and to watch him perform and dance socially. His enthusiastic personality, his knowledge of the history of swing music and dance, and his willingness to share that information made him a popular teacher. He won a Tony Award in 1989 for his choreography for the Broadway revue *Black and Blue*, choreographed *Jumpin' the Blues* for the Alvin Ailey American Dance Theater, created *Swing* for the American Ballroom Theater, choreographed and performed with the Congeroo Dancers in the film *Hellsapoppin'* (1941), choreographed and danced in *Radio City Revels* with Whitey's Hopping Maniacs, collaborated with and performed for Debbie Allen's television movie *Stompin' at the Savoy*, was interviewed for Ken Burns's documentary *Jazz*, and lectured and was the subject of hundreds of articles and books.

During the 1940s, the jitterbug was one of the most popular dances in the United States. A type of swing dance, the jitterbug is performed here by professional dancers Leon James and Willa Mae Ricker in 1942.

"Boogie Woogie Bugle Boy," "American Patrol," and much of the repertory of the orchestras of Glenn Miller, the Dorsey Brothers, and Benny Goodman helped create the big band sound of the 1930s and 1940s and popularized jazz and swing. Their music brought America to soldiers at the front and war themes to Americans back home. The Glenn Miller

Orchestra was one of America's most popular dance bands in the years just before World War II, playing hits such as "Tuxedo Junction," "In the Mood," and "Moonlight Serenade." During the war, Miller joined the army and led the Glenn Miller Army Air Corps Band, which had regular radio broadcasts to America and Europe. Although Millers' plane disappeared over the English Channel in 1944, the Glenn Miller Orchestra is still the most popular big band in the world today for both concert and dance engagements.

The popularity of jazz dancing waned after World War II as the steady danceable rhythm of swing changed into syncopated jazz music and added a more complex bebop beat. As musicians such as Dizzy Gillespie and Charlie Parker improvised more, less melody was apparent, which made jazz better for listening than for dancing. Small jazz bands rather than large swing orchestras and a federal tax on dance floors had a devastating effect on ballrooms. The tax penalized clubs that had entertainment but did not penalize those with music only, so clubs eliminated their dance floors. Although ballroom dance classes taught the steps and teenagers did everything from the jitterbug (Lindy) to the latest dances to the rock 'n' roll songs of the 1960s, it wasn't until the 1980s that the Mama Lu Parks Dancers began reconstruction of the early acrobatic Lindy hop and a group of dancers formed the New York Swing Dance Society.

By the late 1990s, swing dance had regained its popularity. John Waters's musical *Hairspray* introduced swing to another generation. Television commercials for The Gap showed kids swing dancing in khakis, showcasing the excitement of swing to viewers. Swing Web sites such as savoystyle.com, lindyhoppers.com, and yehodi.com have further promoted the dance form.

The Late Twentieth Century

ROCK 'N' ROLL IS HERE TO STAY

The popular music and dance of the 1950s was *rock 'n' roll*, a term coined by disc jockey Alan Freed. While teenage audiences screamed and swooned at the music and the performers, the establishment was against rock 'n' roll, echoing the feelings of past centuries. Clergy and psychiatrists called for bans of music they called obscene and disruptive, fearing it would incite juvenile delinquency, violence, and sex. Radio stations refused to play rock music; some even burned the 45 rpm (rotations per minute) records they received. For a 1958 national television broadcast, Bo Diddley had to refrain, through stipulation of his contract, from moving while he sang in order to "preserve decency." Whenever kids went to concerts, they clapped to the rhythm, yelled, or jumped out of their seats to "groove" in the aisles. Their actions were generally interpreted as "rioting" by authorities. Neither the fans nor the artists were supposed to react naturally to the rhythmic lure of the music.

When hip-shaking Elvis Presley appeared on television, youths adopted his gyrating-pelvis style. Although Presley had been on national television six times, his 1956 appearance on *The Milton Berle Show* triggered the first controversy of his career as he sang "Hound Dog" accompanied by the pelvic grinding his fans loved. Critics across the nation slammed the performance for its vulgarity, animalism, and lack of musicality. The Catholic Church issued "beware Elvis Presley" warnings over concerns that juvenile delinquency and lack of moral values would result from the popular singer.

Although some of his scheduled television appearances were cancelled, he performed three times on the *Ed Sullivan Show* with the cameras showing his image only from the waist up.

Rock music and dance, of course, survived the objections and attacks and entered schools, football stadiums, and malls. The pelvis was never so popular as when teens incorporated Presley's movements into their dancing over the objections of their parents and teachers. The tunes and the dances were enlisted to help sell everything from cars to hamburgers and to lure customers into department stores and supermarkets. Because 45 rpm and LP (long-playing) records were inexpensive, music was readily available to postwar baby boomers who set the tone for dance trends.

ROCK AROUND THE CLOCK

In 1955, Bill Haley and the Comets' song "Rock around the Clock" hit the charts and revived popular dancing, especially for teenagers because dancing was their form of music consumption. The dance craze was fueled by the 150 teenagers from the streets of Philadelphia who danced on *American Bandstand* while top-40 artists sang the music. An expression of youthful energy, the jitterbug (**jive** in England) of the 1940s became rock 'n' roll in the 1950s and 1960s. As the swing era emerged from the big band era, white middle-class America adapted the jitterbug to current music. Although much of its acrobatic, aerial style was subdued, many new steps—crazy legs, stooge jump, flying saucer lift, leg swipes, and wrap—were modified or borrowed from other dances or invented by creative dancers.

Between radio, film, records, the jukebox, and dance parties on television, pop music was available to all. The success of white music (Elvis Presley and Jerry Lee Lewis) with black youth and the success of black artists (Fats Domino and James Brown) with white teenagers signified a definite shift in racial attitudes, although integration in America was still down the road.

The **madison** originated in Baltimore on *The Buddy Deane Show*. It was a dance of two parallel lines facing outward with forward and backward steps, shifting weight, and sweeping feet. Steps from other dances were combined with shuffle, step-clap, tracing letters with the foot, or stylized mime such as batting a ball or shooting a basketball.

LET'S TWIST AGAIN

The twist, danced to Chubby Checker's songs "The Twist" and "Let's Twist Again," was popularized on *American Bandstand*. A fast, frantic dance with no real steps, it could be done in a group or with a partner, although the dancers rarely touched. Chubby Checker claimed that he invented the dance while drying off after a shower. The dance was basically a rotation of the hips in one direction while the knees went the opposite way and the arms moved in counterdirection, or circled. Sometimes done flat-footed, variations included pivoting the ball of the foot with the heel lifted, transferring weight from one foot to the other, and raising one leg while twisting. The dance was an international phenomenom that lasted more than two years and resurfaced to have multi-generation appeal. It was a revolutionary way to dance; couples did not even have to touch. Dancers could face each other or turn their backs on their partners for periods of time, twist the same way or add variations to express individuality or even competitiveness. Critics felt solo dancing was a sign of isolation in a fractured society, but dancers saw themselves as more aware of people around them. As with the Charleston in the 1920s, national competitions were held to find the best twister or the dancer who could outlast the others, reminiscent of early dance marathons. The fad produced 50 single records and 15 albums of twist music; even the Beatles capitalized on the fad with their recording of "Twist and Shout."

In the early 1960s go-go dancing started in New York at the Peppermint Lounge with women dancing the twist on tabletops. Nightclub and discotheque owners hired dancers to entertain their patrons. Soon any

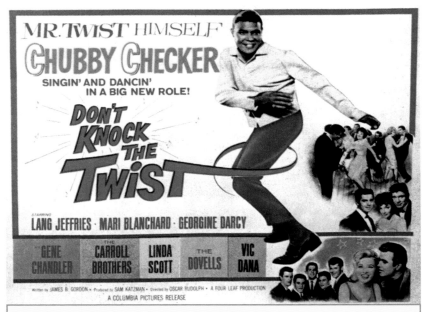

The twist—a fast, frantic dance with no real steps—debuted on the *Dick Clark Show* in August 1960 and quickly became a worldwide phenomenon. The dance was so popular that a movie, *Don't Knock the Twist*, was released in 1962. The plot revolved around a television variety show called *The Twist*.

female wearing a miniskirt with wide a belt, bouffant hairdo (beehive), and knee-high boots (usually white patent leather) was called a *go-go girl*; and teenagers and young adults in their twenties were copying the dance moves. Television took up the idea by having go-go dancers featured on shows such as *Hullabaloo*, *Shivaree*, *That Show of Shows*, and *Shindig*. Although some of the performances were improvised, many had trained dancers doing choreographed routines. Actress/dancer Goldie Hawn made an early appearance as a wild go-go girl on *Laugh-In*. Nancy Sinatra sang her hit song "These Boots Are Made for Walkin'" on television with background dancers in go-go outfits at the height of the fad. In the 1980s, go-go dancing regained popularity and spread to nightclubs throughout the Western world and East Asia with dancers performing on raised platforms or in stylized cages.

TEENS ON TELEVISION

American Bandstand was a television show in which 150 "ordinary" teens from the streets of Philadelphia enjoyed an afternoon record hop (in junior and senior high schools, these were often held in the gymnasium and became "sock hops" in order to protect the basketball courts from street shoes). In 1957, *American Bandstand* went to national syndication. Hosted by Dick Clark, a clean-cut, older brother-type host, the show also promoted musical artists, who were typically lip-synching to their latest release, sometimes while American Bandstand regulars danced. Although early shows were segregated, later shows had both black and white couples dancing, but never integrated couples. Each show featured Clark interviewing teenagers about their opinions of songs being played. More than 100 top-40 artists appeared on the show, which ended in 1989. Thus, television dance shows helped promote record sales and were a means of introducing the latest dances to teens across the nation.

The Buddy Deane Show, a teen show similar to *American Bandstand*, aired on WJZ-TV in Baltimore from 1957 to 1964. The teenagers who appeared on the show every day, known as the "Committee," had a huge following of fans who copied their dance moves and their look and followed their life stories. It was taken off the air because the station was unable to integrate black and white dancers. The show provided the inspiration for John Waters's movie *Hairspray* (1988) starring Divine and Ricki Lake, the Broadway musical with Harvey Fierstein and Marissa Jaret Winokur, and the 2007 movie featuring John Travolta and Nikki Blonsky.

NOVELTY DANCES

Along with rock 'n' roll came dozens of new dance crazes, many of which lasted for less than a year. During a 10-year period, hundreds of novelty dances and their songs dominated teen culture. Pop singers, such as Chubby Checker and Fats Domino, and groups recorded songs such as "Pony Time," "The Twist," "The Locomotion," and "The Monster Mash"—all of which inspired dances by the same names. In the 1960s, scores of new dances (and their accompanying songs) came and went— the **watusi**, the **hully gully**, the monkey, the slop, the mashed potato, and the **stroll**. Those dances, as well as the pony, the jerk, the swim, the boogaloo, the **frug**, the Freddie, and others, were done by every high school student, demonstrating the need for teens to be "hep" to the newest fad and to be part of the "in-crowd." In 1965, the capture of the first uninjured killer whale, Mamu, inspired the creation of a new dance by the same name. These novelty dances taught white teenagers how to do African-based dances; competence doing them represented a form of modernism. A key component of teenage culture was the ability to do the latest dances. These dances departed from the usual social etiquette of partners dancing together, as there was more emphasis on group solidarity, mimicking, and following the movements of others.

The **limbo**, a popular dance at parties during the 1960s, needed only **calypso** music and a six-foot pole held at each end as dancers, one at a time, bent backward and scooted forward, knees flexing lower and lower, to pass under the bar until they were clear. At the start of each round, the pole was lowered further. Participants were eliminated for touching the bar, falling, or failing to clear it completely. The person who could pass under the lowest setting won the competition; a really skilled limbo dancer could pass under a bar 12 inches or less above the floor with his torso nearly parallel to the floor.

RHYTHM, BLUES, AND SOUL

When rhythm and blues combined with **doo-wop** and **gospel**, **soul** music was born. Its greatest exponent was James Brown whose stage act was a mixture of in-your-face entertainment, charisma, revivalist preacher, and innovative dancer. His energetic style drew upon the acrobatic tap dancing of the Nicholas Brothers and vaudeville, sliding across the stage on one foot, spinning, dropping into the splits, and singing on his knees, with microphone in hand. A dance created in New York, called the **good foot**, imitated Brown's theatrical moves while singing "Get on the Good Foot," and his style was copied in the 1980s by break-dancers. Brown influenced dancing both in clubs and on stage, notably in the actions of Michael Jackson and Mick Jagger. Brown's sound and style were popularized by Motown, where the Four Tops and the Temptations were trained to do precision moves while singing, reviving many of the moves of the 1940s such as the camel walk, the Suzy Q, the boogie woogie, and truckin' to accompany their vocals.

In the late 1960s, self-absorption, rejection of societal rules, ecstasy, and free expression were the norm. There was no formal structure to social dancing as people just responded to music by improvising any way they felt like moving. Rock music, flashing lights, and the use of psychedelic (mind-expanding) drugs such as LSD encouraged exhibitionism. The hippies in the Haight-Ashbury section of San Francisco and communes around the country typified the free spirit of the flower children, and the dance and music at Woodstock in 1969 represented the "far out" attitude of youth. Protests and sit-ins were common, drugs to lift depression and raise self-confidence replaced real experience, and rock music was everywhere. Hippie rock fans created their own free society, dancing among the crowds at rock festivals as a way of replacing a "square" culture with a "cool" one. The rock beat that parents thought produced self-indulgence and wayward behavior evolved into diverse forms—**heavy metal**, **punk**, **acid**, and **techno**—and brought about more variations of social dancing.

SATURDAY NIGHT FEVER

Disco was the last craze in music and dance originating with baby boomers. It brought back dancing in contact with a partner. To embrace disco dancing, one only needed 8-track music by the Bee Gees, bell-bottom pants, a tie-dyed shirt, and a partner with lots of imaginative moves. The icon of the 1970s disco culture was undoubtedly John Travolta strutting on the dance floor in white suit, open shirt, one hand pointing up and then crossing the body to point down. In 1977, the movie *Saturday Night Fever* brought disco dancing and the **hustle**, a cross between swing and Latin **merengue**, to mainstream America. Discotheques sprang up overnight with spinning silver balls sending splashes of light around the darkened and crowded dance floor. Spectators might form around a couple with particularly intricate moves. Although the hustle step was simple—side, side, back, front, either in an even or syncopated beat—the spinning of the female along with a variety of arm movements, complicated lifts, and back-to-back or cuddle positions made the dance look intricate. Disco dancing was competitive and narcissistic with couples performing showy routines. Amplified sound, whirling strobe lights, fog machines, mirrors, and fast-paced, rhythm-driven music allowed dancers to hear the beat with their entire bodies. The disc jockey was a central figure, feeling the mood and setting the level and energy of the dancing. Use of drugs such as LSD, marijuana, and Quaaludes and the relentless disco beat contributed to the psychedelic experience.

A number of line dances to hustle music were invented, allowing any number of dancers to take to the dance floor and easily learn the four to five steps that were repeated over and over. These dances included the hustle, the bus stop, and the **electric slide**. Happily, the many variations of disco dancing inspired an upsurge of lessons at dancing schools. Once again, a dance craze revived the dance marathon as well as fashion, music, and even disco roller skating.

In 1978, the Village People recorded a disco classic—"YMCA." It was popular at school dances, camps, and even football games. Everyone sang along with the lyrics while spelling the letters through arm gestures at each chorus. As proof of its lasting popularity, it is done regularly at parties, conventions, and school dances today. In 2008, more than 45,000 spectators in the stands performed "YMCA" at the Sun Bowl in El Paso, Texas.

By the end of the 1970s, punk and **new wave** music were "in" and disco was "out." Small transistor radios followed by portable boom boxes meant music was available everywhere at any time.

As disco dancing became passé, country and western dancing grew in popularity. With the spread (via radio) of country and western music, both line dancing and couple dancing were created, borrowing from

Thanks in part to the movie *Saturday Night Fever*, disco became the most prominent dance in the United States in the late 1970s. Here, actors John Travolta and Karen Lynn Gorney dance in a scene from the movie.

disco. The form lives on in the line dancing popularized in the 1990s and done in clubs and as aerobic exercise. Once again, John Travolta brought a dance form into the mainstream in the movie *Urban Cowboy*, exploring the country western dance scene in honky-tonks. Couple dances have a set form, usually based on the two-step and often choreographed to popular tunes. Choreographed dance sequences make up line dances where dancers face the same direction, do four to six steps, make a quarter turn to face each wall, and then repeat the sequence. Teaching line dancing has become big business, and thousands of dances have been created around the world where country western dancing has attracted a large following of individuals decked out in fringe, sequins, leather, and cowboy boots.

Two dances that emerged in the 1980s are credited with a revival of couples actually dancing together—the lambada with its Brazilian roots and the Cuban-based salsa. Called the forbidden dance, the lambada had spicy lyrics and sexually suggestive movements by dancers pressed tightly together reminiscent of the maxixe. Salsa was actually a nickname created in New York referring to a variety of different music from several Hispanic countries. Danced to a mixture of rhumba, mambo, cha cha cha, merengue, and other Cuban music, salsa used a pattern of six steps danced over eight counts of music, similar to mambo but with more sideways motion. A new generation began to dance together once more in close embrace.

Another popular twentieth-century social dance was **zydeco**, or Cajun. A cultural mix of French-Canadian settlers (Acadians) and Africans who came to Louisiana from the Caribbean islands, Cajuns formed a style with folk dance roots, using heavily syncopated music that originated at the beginning of the twentieth century among the Creoles of southwest Louisiana. The basic step of eight beats has a slow-quick-quick rhythm, with a pause on the second and sixth beats. Variations may be a brush, kick, toe or heel tap, foot twist, or flick with the free (unweighted) foot, known as "eat-a-beat." The feel of the dance has been described as similar to riding a horse or a wagon down the trail, traveling, so couples may two-step it, similar to country western dance, and the two styles are interchangeable. Zydeco can be done in closed or open position, similar to swing, and line dances also are popular. Like many dances in America, zydeco reflects a diverse heritage from the many cultures whose immigrants settled here. Folk dance groups are found everywhere; some specialize in dances of one culture, such as Greece, Ireland, Scandinavia, Eastern Europe, or Israel, or they provide a mixture of many countries.

Dancing in the Millennium

STREET DANCING

Originating with blacks and Latinos in the 1990s, hip-hop includes a variety of styles of dance, including **popping**, **locking**, electric boogie (**electric boogaloo**), b-boying/b-girling (**break dancing**), **house**, krump, and **freaking**. These informal and improvisational urban street dances were social expressions wrapped up in movement, text (rap), and sound (boom box). Even though hip-hop was often linked with guns, violence, and death, it could also present a moral, regenerative message and express individuality. The collective energy of the communal circle surrounding the soloist served as support for the dancers and as a socializing process. A source of energy and joy, hip-hop began as a spiritual antidote to oppression, alienation, and depression. Rap artists who danced while rapping, such as MC Hammer and Salt-N-Pepa, helped spread hip-hop through videos.

Initially a solo street dance in which breakers took turns showing off, hip-hop was a competition, which has evolved into recreation or a concert showpiece. The exploration of body parts moving in isolation, the freeze, rapid shifting footwork, acrobatics and flips, sharp weight

A group of break-dancers perform in Brooklyn, New York, in 1984. Break dancing, or b-boying/b-girling, originated on the streets of the Bronx, New York, in the 1970s as a social expression wrapped up in movement, text (rap), and sound (boom box).

changes, and spinning on the back or head demonstrate youthful vitality, vigor, and strength. Unlike the verticality of classical dance (ballet, modern, jazz), hip-hop uses a horizontal body, dissonance, and ragged gesture juxtaposed with a cool, relaxed, laid-back attitude. It has borrowed steps from jazz, gymnastics, and even **capoiera**, a Brazilian tradition that blends dance with martial arts. Popping and locking emphasize robotic posturing and isolated motions of the joints—waves, punches, shoulder hikes, and the **coffee grinder**.

Rave was first used in the 1980s to describe extended dance parties, often lasting all night, with DJs playing fast electronic music and orchestrating light shows; R-A-V-E is an acronym for "radical audio visual experience" in which synthesizers create a trancelike sound. By the end of the 1980s, rave often described the acid subculture in which parties were an excuse to use street drugs such as cocaine, ecstasy, and amphetamines. Not unlike at parties in the late 1960s, the dancing was freestyle, a personal emotional response to the various styles of sound including techno, hardcore, tribal, jungle, and house.

Krump is a style invented in the early 1990s in Los Angeles by Tommy the Clown, who used a series of wild comedic gestures to entertain kids at parties. This "clowning" evolved to "**krumping**," used in rough areas of at-risk kids as an alternative to joining gangs. This freestyle body motion has rhythm and coordination but no set moves. It involves chest popping, comedic fast-paced Charlie Chaplin moves, staccato strides, stumbling, toe dance, torso waves, body jerking, and prancing. Krump should tell a story. It can be aggressive, angry, seductive, comedic, sensual, or emotional.

Other late twentieth-century dance forms include **stepping**—a rhythmic, unison style of street dance made popular by African-American fraternities—and **vogueing**—a vernacular dance form, popularized by Madonna but originating in clubs in New York City. It imitates fashion model poses. Television, rather than theater, is the medium that has spread this new dance culture; urban street dances feed on television music and dance as well as the reverse.

A TELEVISION IN EVERY HOME

The speed with which new dance fads have swept the United States can be attributed to television. Dance shows of the 1960s to 1980s were instrumental in promoting new dances, new steps, and the music that accompanied them, such as the 1970s disco show *Dance Fever* (and its revival in 2003). Public television began to air professional and amateur ballroom dance competitions, including U.S. and international championships and its 2006 *America's Ballroom Challenge*. When cable television provided dozens (now hundreds) of channels to watch and reality television took over the airwaves, programs specific to dance were developed to catch the attention of the public. One of the most popular, *Dancing with the Stars*, which pairs a ballroom dance champion with a celebrity, has encouraged thousands of Americans to take social dance lessons. Versions of the show are licensed in 30 countries. In the

American tradition of "if one is good, more must be better" other shows have attempted to copy its success, including *Ballroom Bootcamp*, *So You Think You Can Dance*, *Dance Your Ass Off*, *Dance Revolution*, *Step It Up and Dance*, and even *Skating with Celebrities*, pairing celebrities with professional figure skaters. Riding on the success of *Dancing with the Stars*, in 2008 two of its judges produced the face-off series, *Dance War: Bruno vs. Carrie Ann*. Two DVDs, *Dancing with the Stars: Cardio Dance* (2007) and *Latin Cardio* (2008); a book, *Dancing with the Stars: Jive, Samba, & Tango Your Way into the Best Shape in Your Life*; and a line of workout clothing are on the market. In addition, the dancers are featured in tours around the country at major theaters.

MUSIC TELEVISION

In 1981, Music Television (MTV) created musical and visual innovations that over time promoted pop stars, such as Madonna, Michael Jackson, and Ricky Martin. MTV also encouraged the sales of the pop music they featured on TV and disseminated new dance steps for public consumption. Cable and satellite stations were able to create programs aimed at the youth market. The interaction of image, sound, and choreography impacted the viewers on several levels that led them to purchase the recordings. Music videos created dance crazes or used them to sell pop music singles. The 24-hour station MTV broadcasted nonstop musical video clips and transformed the pop music entertainment industry.

Michael Jackson's videos used street dance moves, including his trademark kicks, spins, pelvic thrusts, and moonwalking.[31] Both his videos *Bad* and *Beat It* take place on the street with ordinary people dancing and Jackson showcased as the "star." Jackson successfully used underground street styles and made them mainstream pop. His 14-minute *Thriller* had all the trappings of a Hollywood movie musical—ambitious choreography, storyline, rehearsal, and high production costs. In 1989, the entertainment industry named *Thriller* "the greatest video in the history of the world."[32] With Jackson's premature death, *Thriller* has become an industry in itself, including an attempt to make the *Guinness Book of World Records* by having thousands of dancers around the world dance the *Thriller* routine at the same hour on the same day.

Michael Jackson performs the moonwalk during the HIStory World Tour in December 1996. The moonwalk, synonymous with the pop icon, is a back-sliding dance that gives the illusion of the dancer being pulled backward while attempting to move forward.

Madonna—singer, dancer, fashion icon, actress—borrowed dance styles of the day, for example, vogueing in her song "Vogue" (1985), the lavish style of earlier Hollywood film musicals in "Material Girl" (1990), and krumping in "Hung Up" (2005). These dance styles demonstrated her ability to appropriate street culture, repackage social dance styles, innovate, and sell a song—a hybrid of pop concert and musical theater. Using music video, Madonna created a screen persona and has repeatedly reinvented herself. On her stage tours, she features innovative choreography and polished routines to sell her music. Similarly, Ricky Martin used a backdrop of dancers doing moves from Latin American social dances to link his artistry and music with the "hot" Latin style.

Thus, as with dance during the previous 400 years, popular dance innovations and appropriations flowed back and forth between professional entertainers and everyday people, in this case between street, stage, and music videos.

In the mid-1990s, another Latin dance made it to America. Invented in Venezuela, the **macarena** became the "in" line dance at parties. Each measure of music called for various hand gestures or hands to be placed on opposite shoulders, hips, or buttocks. Each chorus of music ended with a pelvic rotation and a one-quarter jumping turn. It was even danced at both the Democratic and Republican National Conventions in 1996. As with other novelty dances, its popularity was short lived, though it is resurrected from time to time at parties.

Freaking—a dance that some find offensive—originated in the mid-1990s. Usually done to rhythm and blues, hip-hop, or rap music—often to sexually explicit songs with graphic movements—it may also be called grinding, booty dancing, or **bump and grind**. Performed with multiple partners, most adults feel it simulates sexual violence, particularly with boys grabbing girls from behind. Many people who dance it insist that it is just grooving to the music with no sexual intention, but some parents continue to be horrified by freaking and some school systems have banned students from doing it at school-sponsored dances.

The ultimate mass reaction to movement and rhythm may well be found in football, basketball, soccer, and baseball stadiums, where thousands of fans perform "the wave" in perfect synchronization with no rehearsal and no direction. Fans in each section stand and raise their arms, then sit down as each section repeats the movement sequentially so that the wave rolls around the stands. This is sport's equivalent to dancing and allows fans to be a part of the action and move rhythmically as a group. In addition, songs such as "Who Let the Dogs Out?" and "We Will Rock You" keep the stands rocking and the fans swaying. Even grounds crews at Yankee Stadium have been seen dancing to "YMCA" as they sweep the infield.

BALLROOM GOES TO HOLLYWOOD, AGAIN

Although ballroom dancing has made its appearance in movies since the 1920s—as background for a scene or for furthering the plot—it has also been the theme of many films—*They Shoot Horses Don't They*, *Last Tango in Paris*, *Dirty Dancing*, *Strictly Ballroom*, *Dance with Me*, and *Shall We Dance* (a Japanese film followed a few years later by a version with an American cast). The movies *Breakin'* and *Beat Street* celebrated break dancing, and *Wild Style* and *Flashdance* brought hip-hop into the mainstream. Dance on film has done more than just attract people to the theater or send the masses rushing out to practice new steps. Extravagant routines have given a more sophisticated public a method to tell a story.

DanceSport describes competitive ballroom dancing, a term invented to lure the International Olympic Committee to accept ballroom dancing as an Olympic sport. It requires serious study for amateurs and professionals to master the steps and levels of proficiency (bronze, silver, gold). Two major divisions comprise DanceSport competitions held throughout five continents—standard (waltz, Viennese waltz, foxtrot, quickstep, tango) and Latin[33] (samba, rhumba, cha cha, paso doble, jive). Its requirement for discipline and practice combined with a glamorous image bring it closer to athletic competition and farther from popular social dancing. While dances and nightclubs provide fun, recreation, frivolity, spontaneity, and sociability, DanceSport is serious and requires the commitment of long hours of rehearsal of choreography as well as financial investment (shoes can cost more than $200, dresses more than

$800). Parties and clubs in the Latin community offer friendship, romance, and emotional honesty, while DanceSport brings recognition, awards, and financial success to professional competitors. It is a theatrical presentation of social dance with visual effects, dynamics, speed, control, tricks, and showmanship. The effect on the viewers (including the judges) is the most important thing, while the exchange between partners, self-indulgence, enjoyment, and feeling the moves drive the social dancer.

ELECTRONIC MEDIA

In the late twentieth century, various styles of social dance became the subject of "how-to" videos; they were also adopted for workout videos. Jazz, Latin, tap, and belly dancing—nearly every dance style has lent itself to a video, and many have become choreographed into aerobic dance workouts. In the twenty-first century, **zumba**—aerobic dancing to Latin music—is the new craze. MTV shows the latest bands, singers, dancers, and star-making competitions. One can view an endless array of dance on DVDs; the Internet provides short excerpts of dance on YouTube; and entire shows, such as *Dancing with the Stars*, can be viewed on network Web sites. Dance has never been so accessible; however, one hopes that people will actually DO it, not just watch it.

There is no doubt that media—dance manuals, newspapers, magazines, radio, film, audio recordings, and MTV—have shaped the style and fostered the popularity of social and theatrical dancing for the last five centuries. The media have also determined how dances have been "sold" to the public, whether as popular dance for doing or popular dance for watching. Social and theatrical dances are linked and have helped develop social mores, etiquette, behavior, and peer acceptance. In addition, they define a person's place in society. Social and theatrical dance forms and styles exchange with one another, and a creative loop between choreographers, dancers, and the general public allows for transmission, recycling, transformation, and an endless variety of versions. The social dances created in the twenty-first century will become dance traditions in the future.

Once merely entertainment and recreation, ballroom dancing has gained distinction in the quest for better health; research in the early twenty-first century shows its potential not only as a fitness activity but as a means to ward off senility and Alzheimer's. Numerous clinical studies have shown that the benefits of a regular program of ballroom dancing—the mentally and physically challenging aspects of following complex dance steps, moving in time and staying with the rhythm of music, and social interaction—are associated with a lowered risk of dementia. A study, published in the June 2003 issue of the *New England Journal of Medicine*, found that ballroom dancing outperformed all the activities evaluated (swimming, biking, group exercises); dance was the only one associated with a lower risk of the age-related cognitive decline. The ballroom dancers in the study reduced their risk of dementia by an amazing 76 percent. Ballroom dancing takes center stage for keeping the mind sharp and makes a longer life worth living.

CHRONOLOGY

Thirteenth–Fourteenth Centuries	Basse danse, branle, estampie, danse macabre, May dances, and sword dances are developed.
Fourteenth Century	Morris dancing evolves as ritual and entertainment.
Fifteenth Century	Canary, hey, hornpipe, and moresque are developed.
1463	Domenico da Piacenza publishes treatise on dance, *De arte saltandi and choreas ducendi.*
Sixteenth Century	Allemande, bourreé, chaconne, cinq pas, country dance, courante, galliard, measure, pavane, sarabande, Sir Roger de Coverly, and la volta are developed.
1507	Danse macabre is performed as masque at Tuscan court.
1565	Catherine de Médicis brings French provincials to court to entertain the nobles—an early performance.
1577	Caroso writes treatise on dance, *Il Ballarino.*
1581	Balthazar de Beaujoyeulx choreographs *Ballet Comique de la Reine* for Catherine de Médicis.
1588	*Orchesographie* is published by Thoinot Arbeau.

Seventeenth Century	Contredanse, flamenco, gavotte, gigue, passacaglia, and rigaudon are developed.
1602	Cezare Negri produces *Le Grazie d'Amore*.
1604	Negri's book is republished under the title *New Invention of the Ballet*.
1612	*Carrousel du Roi* is choreographed by Antoine de Pluvinel for the marriage of Louis XIII.
1619	The first African slaves arrive in America.
1620	Puritans arrive in Plymouth, Massachusetts.
1632	The first ballet in a theater is performed for a paying audience.
1651	John Playford publishes *The English Dancing Master or Plaine and Easie Rules for the Dancing of Country Dances, with the Tune to Each Dance*.
1653	Louis XIV appears as Apollo in Benserade's *Ballet de la Nuit*.
1661	Académie Royale de Musique et Danse is established by Louis XIV.
1670	The minuet (menuet) is adopted by the French.
1671	Pierre Beauchamps is appointed as Louis XIV's ballet master.
1681	*The Hunt of Diana* is performed in 23 acts.
	Women first appear on stage in a public theater.
1684	Increase Mather's *An Arrow Against Profane and Promiscuous Dancing, Drawne Out of the Quiver of the Scriptures* is published in Boston.
1685	The first dancing masters travel throughout the colonies teaching children and adults.

Eighteenth Century	Appalachian mountain dancing, contras, cotillion, minuet, passepied, English country dancing, jigs, hornpipe, and Scottish reels are developed.
1700	The first book about dance notation is published by Feuillet: *Choreography or the Art of Describing the Dance*.
1701	Feuillet publishes *Choreography of the Art of Acting and Dance for Characters, Figures, and Mimes*.
1721	John Weaver writes *Anatomy and Mechanical Lectures upon Dancing*.
1725	Rameau writes *Le Maitre a Danser* (*The Dancing Master*).
1735	Kellom Tomlinson publishes *The Art of Dancing*.
1739	Laws are passed in British colonies in America forbidding blacks to use drums—a native instrument—out of fear they will arouse slaves to insurrection.
1770	Cotillion comes to the British colonies in America from Europe.
1774	The Continental Congress passes a resolution prohibiting public balls, but it does not end them.
	Two dancing teachers, Pietro Sodi and Signor Tioli, establish schools in Philadelphia.
1775	The Revolutionary War begins in America at Concord, Massachusetts; it ends in 1783.
1776	The Declaration of Independence is signed.
1782	Frenchman Louis Roussell begins teaching social dancing in Baltimore, Maryland.

1785   John Durang first dances a hornpipe in the United States.

Dancing master Monsieur Roussel introduces the Pigeon Wing to polite society in Philadelphia.

1788   John Griffith publishes the first dance book in the United States: *A Collection of the Newest and Most Fashionable Country Dances and Cotillions, the Great Part by Mr. John Griffith, Dancing Master, in Providence.*

French reinforcements arrive in the United States; numerous balls of minuets entertain officers.

1790   John Durang, first American professional dancer, makes his stage debut with the Old American Theatre Company at the Baltimore Theatre.

The French Revolution ends court dancing and the noble style.

1791   Alexander Placide comes to the United States and dances a hornpipe on a tightrope.

Pierre Tastel, a French dancing master, establishes an academy of dance in Charleston, South Carolina.

French dancer Alexander Placide arrives in Charleston and becomes manager of the Charleston Theatre.

1794   Mme. Gardie, a dancer from Santo Domingo, appears in *Le For'et Noire* at the New Theatre in Philadelphia.

1796   James Byrne, an English dancer and mime whose specialty is Harlequin, makes his American debut in Philadelphia in the grand serious pantomime, *The Death of Captain Cook,* with Native Dancers of the Hawaiian Islands.

Nineteenth Century   The Bolero, galop, Lancers quadrille, mazurka, polka, polonaise schottische, waltz, can can, habañera, milonga, redowa round dance, square dance, two-step, varsouvienne, and cakewalk are developed.

1808   Thomas Wilson publishes *An Analysis of Country Dancing.*

1815   The quadrille is brought to England from France.

1816   The quadrille arrives in the United States.

1828   Thomas Dartmouth (Daddy) Rice presents *Jump Jim Crow* characterization (the forerunner of the Negro image depicted throughout the minstrel era) for the first time at the Columbia Street Theatre in Cincinnati, Ohio.

1830   The hula is officially banned in Hawaii.

1832   Italian musician and dancer Signor Papanti establishes a dancing school on Boston's Tremont Row and is appointed master of deportment and dancing at West Point.

1840   The hula is reinstated as the national dance of Hawaii.

Juba and minstrelsy begins.

The polka from Czechoslovakia arrives in the United States.

1843   Polkamania begins in Paris.

1845–1852   The potato famine in Ireland drives Irish immigrants to the United States along with their jigs, reels, and clog dances.

1847   John Durang's *Terpsichore,* or *Ballroom Guide,* is published in Philadelphia.

1848   Juba (William Henry Lane) travels to London to perform with a blackface minstrel troupe, Pell's Ethiopian Serenaders.

1861–1865   The War between the States (Civil War) is fought in America.

1866   The *Black Crook* (considered the first "musical comedy") opens in Niblo's Garden Theatre in New York City.

1870–1935   Vaudeville brings popular dance to the stage and gives new dances to the public.

1884   George E. Wilson publishes *Wilson's Ball-room Guide and Call Book, or Dancing Self-Taught*.

1885   Allen Dodworth publishes *Dancing and Its Relation to Education and Social Life with a New Method of Instruction Including a Complete Guide to the Cotillion (German) with 250 Figures*.

1893   The Negro dance the cakewalk becomes an international craze.

1895   Arthur Murray is born.

1897   William & Walker perform their musical extravaganza.

1900   Carnivals, gillies, and other tent shows begin to disintegrate in favor of vaudeville theater.

1905   Juilliard School of Music is founded in New York City.

1907   Cecil Sharp publishes his first *Morris Books*.

1910   The grizzly bear, Cubanola slide, and Argentine tango appear in the United States.

1911   The English Folk Dance Society is founded by Cecil Sharp.

The Gabby glide, turkey trot, Texas Tommy, and one-step appear.

1911–1914   Vernon and Irene Castle make ballroom dances respectable.

1912   The camel walk and bunny hug become popular.

1913   *Darktown Follies* opens at the Lafayette Theater in Harlem, New York.

The foxtrot and ballin' the jack appear.

1914   Pope Pius X bans the tango and turkey trot.

The finale of the *Dark Town Follies* added to the *Ziegfeld Follies*.

Hesitation waltz, Castle walk, Castle glide, maxixe, and Boston become the vogue.

1914–1918   World War I takes place.

1915   Kangaroo hop, horse trot, lame duck, and whirlwind waltz make the scene.

1921   The Charleston first appears in the show *Shuffle Along* (the first musical revue written and performed by African Americans) in Harlem, New York; Josephine Baker's career as a star is launched.

Rudolph Valentino dances a tango in the film *The Four Horsemen of the Apocalypse*.

1922   Fred and Adele Astaire achieve national fame in *For Goodness Sake,* a Broadway show written especially for them.

Lincoln Gardens dance hall in Chicago hires King Oliver's Creole Jazz Band to play New Orleans jazz; Louis Armstrong joins the band.

1923   The Cotton Club opens in New York with all African-American performers and white audiences (closes in 1936).

First documented dance marathon is held in the United States.

The *Ziegfeld Follies of 1923* introduces the Charleston to "society."

1924   Louis Armstrong comes to New York to join the Fletcher Henderson Orchestra at the Roseland Ballroom.

1925   Arthur Murray first franchises dance lessons.

Josephine Baker introduces the Charleston to Paris nightclubs.

1926   The black bottom is introduced by Ann Pennington in George White's show *Scandals*.

The Savoy Ballroom opens in New York, becoming the major ballroom for social dancing, such as the Lindy and Charleston.

The Lindy hop and sugar foot stomp are popular.

1927   The varsity drag is introduced by Zelda O'Neil in *Good News*.

Duke Ellington brings his band to the Cotton Club.

1928   Bill "Bojangles" Robinson gains recognition as a master tap dancer in *Blackbirds*.

1930   The shag, continental, and carioca are popular.

Frankie Manning begins his Lindy career at the Savoy Ballroom.

1932   *Flying Colors,* a Broadway show with separate black and white choruses, opens; it is the first show to hire both racial groups.

1933   Fred Astaire and Ginger Rogers star in their first film together, *Flying Down to Rio.*

Ruby Keeler is the featured dancer in Busby Berkeley's *Gold Diggers of 1933*.

1933–1939 Fred Astaire and Ginger Rogers appear together in 10 films.

1934 The rhumba arrives in the United States from Cuba. There, the spelling is changed to rumba.

1935 George Balanchine choreographs the *Ziegfeld Follies*.

Truckin', Suzy Q, gazin' the fog, jump back jack, and scarecrow are added to Lindy hop.

1936 The jitterbug makes its appearance as a variation of Lindy.

1937 The Lambeth walk first appears in the musical *Me and My Girl*.

1938 The big apple is popularized by Arthur Murray.

1939 The samba and conga come to the United States; the polka is revived.

1941 The hokey-pokey is invented.

1941–1945 The United States takes part in World War II.

1949 The mambo comes to the United States from Cuba.

1950–1960 *The Arthur Murray Party* is broadcast on prime-time television.

1950 The cha cha cha arrives in the United States.

1951 The merengue, fish, watusi, and locomotion begin to be seen on the dance floor.

1952 The bunny hop and madison become popular line dances.

1953 The creep, dirty dog, frug, jerk, and surfer stomp appear.

1955 Bill Haley and the Comets' song "Rock around the Clock" hits the charts—generally considered the begining of the rock 'n' roll era.

The stroll, monkey, shake, and pony make their appearance.

Pérez Prado's "Cherry Pink and Apple Blossom White" helps popularize the cha cha cha.

1957 *American Bandstand* begins its national syndication.

1957–1964 *The Buddy Deane Show* airs in Baltimore.

1958 The Savoy Ballroom closes.

1960 Bossa nova arrives in the United States; the Freddie and the bug are popular.

1960s New dance crazes are invented: the hully gully, monkey, slop, mashed potato, and stroll.

1961 The twist appears on *American Bandstand*.

1974–1980 Disco is popularized by the entertainment industry and dominates the airwaves and the club scene.

1975 Van McCoy writes and releases the song "Do the Hustle."

1977 The movie *Saturday Night Fever* brings disco dancing and the hustle to the public.

1977–1979 Street parties with dance music and rapping DJs become increasingly popular in the New York area and begin the street dance craze.

1978 The Village People record a disco classic: "YMCA."

1982 American Ballroom Company begins conducting the United States Ballroom Championships.

1983   Michael Jackson performs the moonwalk (called "the backslide" in popping context) on ABC's *Motown Special*, which is broadcast throughout the world.

The movie *Flashdance* is released and becomes the first Hollywood film to feature b-boying/b-girling.

1984   The films *Breakin'* and *Breakin' 2: Electric Boogaloo* open internationally and contribute to the exposure of popping, breaking, locking, and electric boogaloo.

The American Ballroom Theater Company is founded.

1985   *Tango Argentino* opens on Broadway.

1986   The movie *Dirty Dancing*, starring Patrick Swayze, is released.

1988   Director John Waters's movie *Hairspray* repopularizes the jitterbug.

1992   The film *Strictly Ballroom* is released.

1997   The International Olympic Committee recognizes DanceSport as an Olympic sport (but not a medal sport).

2002   *Hairspray* opens on Broadway.

Twyla Tharp's *Moving Out*, the all-dance musical set to Billy Joel's music, opens on Broadway.

2003   *Dancing with the Stars* first airs on TV.

2005   The documentary *Mad Hot Ballroom* is released.

2006   PBS airs *America's Ballroom Challenge*.

Take the Lead, a movie starring Antonio Banderas, depicts Pierre Dulaine's efforts to utilize ballroom dancing to help New York City youth.

2007   The University of East London Institute for Performing Arts (IPAD) begins the only BA dance degree program in the world to specialize in hip-hop, urban, and global dance forms.

2008   *Simply Ballroom* begins its U.S. tour starring Debbie Reynolds and a cast of world-class dance champions.

2009   World International Style Ballroom Standard Championships are held in Tokyo, Japan.

Michael Jackson dies in June; 22,596 people in 32 countries dance on October 25 to *Thriller* in the Michael Jackson tribute *Thrill the World*.

2010   *Dancing with the Stars* begins its tenth season on TV.

NOTES

CHAPTER 1

1 *Pyrrhic*—Greek weapon/war dances.

2 *Gymnopaidiai* (*gymnopaedia, gymnopaediae*)—Ancient Greek festival dances to honor Apollo based on the motions of wrestling; also war dancing to show athletic skill and to train Spartan youth in strength, endurance, and musical grace.

3 William Shakespeare, *Much Ado about Nothing* (Act II, Scene I).

4 King James I, "Book of Sports." Encyclopædia Britannica Online. Available online at *http://www. britannica.com/EBchecked/ topic/561039/Book-of-Sports* (accessed December 16, 2009).

5 *Cinq pas*—A step in which the dancer hops on one foot while the other leg makes four kicks to right and left, ending with a cadence (high jump landing on both feet in fourth position).

6 Longways—A progressive dance of couples held in long and narrow assembly rooms (long gallery). Dancers would gather in two lines and face each other. It was a feature of most seventeenth-century country houses.

CHAPTER 2

7 Quoted in Curt Sachs, *World History of the Dance* (New York: W.W. Norton & Company, 1963) 407.

8 *Rigaudon/rigadoon*—A lively seventeenth-century French Baroque folk dance for couples; also the name of a dance step. In Scotland, the seventeenth-century rigaudon was the dance performed by Highland soldiers on the

cross blades of swords with elegant posture, lightness, strength, and catlike use of the feet. Learned at the court of France, the style and steps were later borrowed by ballet dancers.

9 All women's roles were danced by men until 1681.

10 *Commedia D'ell Arte*—Traveling plays developed from Roman theater; these plays were filled with satire, farce, song, dance, and mime.

CHAPTER 3

11 *Richmond Dancing Assemblies* [manuscript collection, 1790s], Virginia Historical Society.

12 William Storrs Lee, *The Yankees of Connecticut* (New York: Henry Holt, 1957), 200–203.

13 William Prynne, *Histrio-Mastix: The Player's Scourge; or, Actor's Tragedy*, 1632. Available online at http://*www.sdean.net/HistrioMastix.html*.

14 Henry R. Stiles, *Ancient Windsor, Connecticut*, 2 vols. (Hartford, CT: Lockwood & Brainard, 1891), 679.

15 Princess Radziwill, *They Knew the Washingtons* (Indianapolis, IN: Bobbs-Merrill Company, 1926), 84–85.

16 George Washington Parke Custis, *Recollections and Private Memoirs* (New York: Derby and Jackson, 1860), 144.

17 William Spohn Baker, *Washington after the Revolution* (Philadelphia: J.B. Lippencott, 1892), 299.

18 John F. Stegeman and Janet A. Stegeman, *Caty: A Biography of Catherine Littlefield Greene* (Athens: University of Georgia Press, 1977), 68.

19 John Durang, *The Memoir of John Durang: American Actor, 1785–1816*, Alan S. Downer, ed. (Pittsburgh, PA: University of Pittsburgh Press, 1966), 11.

20 Nicholas Cresswell, *The Journal of Nicholas Cresswell, 1774–1777* (New York: Dial Press, 1924), 53.

CHAPTER 4

21 Hemoni, "To Parents," *Times and Seasons* 4 (1844): 486.

22 John A. Widstoe, ed., *The Discourses of Brigham Young* (Salt Lake City, UT: Deseret Book, 1925), 374.

CHAPTER 5

23 George E. Wilson, *Wilson's Ball-room Guide and Call Book, or, Dancing Self-Taught* (New York: Excelsior, 1884).

24 Thomas Wilson, *An Analysis of Country Dancing*, 3rd ed. (London: J. S. Dickson, 1811), 39.

25 Lynne F. Emery, *Black Dance in the United States, 1619–1970* (Palo Alto, CA: National Press Books, 1980), 91.

26 Robert De Valcourt, *The Illustrated Manners Book* (New York: Leland Clay, 1855), 407.

CHAPTER 6

27 Henry Rowe Schoolcraft, *The Indian in His Wigwam or Characteristics of the Red Race of America* (New York: W.H. Graham, 1848), 195.

28 George Horse Capture, *Powwow* (Cody, WY: Buffalo Bill Historic Museum, 1989).

CHAPTER 7

29 Irene Castle, *Castles in the Air* (New York: Doubleday, 1958), 31.

30 Rheta Louise Childe Dorr, *What Eight Million Women Want* (Boston: Small, Maynard, 1910; New York: Kraus Reprint, 1971), 209–210.

CHAPTER 11

31 *Moonwalking*, often credited to James Brown and later to Michael Jackson, was actually performed by James Cagney in the Busby Berkeley 1933 film *Footlight Parade* but has its roots in an earlier African-American minstrel dance, called the Virginia essence.

32 Mike Celizic, "'Thriller' Video Remains a Classic 25 Years Later." Available online at *http://www.msnbc.msn.com/id/24282347/* and *www.rockonthenet.com/archive/1999/mtv100.htm.*

33 This category was once called Latin and American, but it was shortened to Latin, hence the confusion as to why jive is a part of the category.

GLOSSARY

acid   Music born out of the use of LSD (aka acid) and other psychedelic drugs with few lyrics, long instrumental solos, improvisation, often accompanied by flashing or strobe lights, that served as background music for acid trips. Acid rock groups include the Doors and the Grateful Dead.

allemande   An arm-intertwining dance popular in France in the mid-1700s; it is a movement in English country dancing in which couples cross arms on each others' backs while turning shoulder to shoulder. In American square dance, it is a progression of pulling past the opposite sex (called rights and lefts in English country dancing).

animal dances   Popular ragtime dances imitating animals such as the turkey trot, kangaroo rag, grizzly bear, chicken scratch, bullfrog hop, possum trot, snake hips, eagle rock, lame duck, and bunny hug; for example, to do the eagle rock, dancers stretched out their arms like an eagle and swayed the torso back and forth.

Ashanti   A major ethnic group in Ghana whose religious beliefs are a mixture of spiritual and supernatural, including ancestors, higher gods, and a supreme being

balance and swing   Common figure in contra dance where couples step left/kick right, and then step right/kick left followed by a "swing your partner"—a stationary turn in closed ballroom position

ballin' the jack   An African-American jazz dance with hip and body movements but no footwork, made famous by its appearance in the musical *Runnin' Wild* (1923)

ballroom dances   Dances usually performed by couples, in a social setting—restaurant, dance hall, assembly, ballroom, or any place set up with

131

a dance floor; the dances include the foxtrot, waltz, tango, rhumba, swing, mambo, samba, salsa, hustle, bossa nova, cha cha, polka, Lindy/jitterbug/swing, and merengue.

barn dances   The product of colonial settlers who modified English country dances; they were performed in halls and barns as get-togethers among America's first settlers in the West.

Baroque   An era (seventeenth to mid-eighteenth centuries) of artistic grandeur, richness, drama, vitality, movement, tension, emotional energy, and the blurring of distinctions between the various arts

basse danse   A dignified, grand, restrained solemn court dance usually in duple time, often done in a procession; it was popular in the fifteenth and sixteenth centuries.

Beauchamps, Pierre   French ballet dancer, choreographer, and teacher to Louis XIV, who appointed him to direct the Académie Royale de Danse in 1661; he composed many court ballets and defined the five basic positions of the feet in ballet.

belly dance   Middle Eastern dance form practiced by women to strengthen the abdominal muscles and aid childbirth. In the Western world, belly dancing has become a form of exhibition dancing in clubs and restaurants and also exercise or workout and to help women feel empowered and good about their bodies.

big apple   A novelty dance of the 1930s and 1940s, made popular by Arthur Murray, in which dancers in a circle respond to instructions called out by a leader

black bottom   An African-American dance of the 1920s; it is made up of single or double stamps, swaying, a slap on the backside, and an occasional kick.

blues   Music genre reflecting melancholy and sadness created by African Americans in the 1890s from ballads, spirituals, and chants commonly using a 12-bar chord progression

boogie woogie   Originally a style of music that became an African-American jazz dance; it had its roots in rock 'n' roll in the 1950s; the dancer travels forward with hips swaying and knees together.

bossa nova   A Brazilian dance from the early 1960s; it was danced to music such as "The Girl from Ipanema" and originated in cafes of Rio de

Janeiro; it combined samba and jazz movements in a fluid, sensuous slow, quick, quick rhythm.

Boston   A slow, easy-going, and less vigorous version of the waltz; it was popular in the early twentieth century.

bourreé   A fast, light, and gay folk dance done in double file with a line of men facing a line of women

branle (also *brawl, brando*)   A balancing motion with chainlike joining of hands and sideward movement of dancing couples in open file or closed circle; it originated with peasants in the Middle Ages.

break dancing   A street dance style (b-boying/b-girling) originating in New York City in the 1970s; it is an athletic mix of freezing, rapidly shifting footwork, acrobatics and flips, sharp weight changes, spinning on the back or head, and sharp percussive movements in response to hip-hop, particularly rap, music.

buck and wing   Early tap dance step originating with Irish step dancing; it uses steps on the balls of the feet (called wings). A combination of buck dancing and pigeon wing, similar to clogging using the heel and toe, it is also called flat footing, hoedown, jigging, sure footing. Pigeon wing was a step done by minstrel and vaudeville dancers—shaking one foot in the air or shooting one foot out to make a wing with arm flapping like a bird's wings.

bump   A dance popular during the disco craze of the 1970s in which dancers bump their hips against their partners' hips on the downbeat of the music

bump and grind   Hip rotations based on the bump, done with one or several partners

cakewalk   A strutting dance of elaborate steps and attitudes invented by African slaves to mock the pretensions of their masters; it later appeared on stage in minstrel shows and was danced socially as a competition, the prize—a cake—going to the best, most inventive dancers.

caller   One who cues the dancers as to the figure(s) to do during a dance, usually in contra, English country, and square dancing; she/he may or may not be dancing at the same time.

calypso   A form of Afro-Caribbean music originating in Trinidad played on guitar, banjo, and steel drums; it was used as a means of communication between slaves and for entertainment. The most popular recording artist of

Calypso music was Harry Belafonte with songs such as "The Banana Boat Song" and "Yellow Bird" (which were also perfect tunes for the cha cha).

canary   A Spanish dance consisting of wild, exotic skips, hops, leaps, and turns combined with heel and sole stamping popular in European courts during the sixteenth century

can can   Scandalous acrobatic dance involving high kicking, jumping into the splits, and quick turning done in French music halls by courtesans or semiprofessional dancers

capoeira   Traditional Brazilian dance combining martial arts and dance steps that is acrobatic and vigorous

Castle lame duck waltz   A syncopated waltz with a limping step that transitioned the dancers from one waltz style to another

Castle walk   A dance comprising a series of elegant walking steps on the toes, punctuated with a small hop during the musical phase; it was first demonstrated at the Cafe de Paris in France by Irene and Vernon Castle in 1913, who introduced it to New York society in 1914.

ceili   Dances formed by Irish dancing masters based on French quadrilles and group set dances; it is also the name of a dance party of Irish dancing.

cha cha cha   Latin dance from Cuba derived from the mambo in 1953 and using a triple step (quick-quick-quick- slow-slow); although cha cha (two chas) is actually a religious dance, the social dance cha cha cha was shortened to only cha cha.

Charleston   Popular dance of the 1920s originating in speakeasies and characterized by pivoting on the feet while flicking of the lower leg and kicking; it was embellished with typical show moves in a 1921 Ziegfeld Follies production.

chassé ("to chase")   Sideways traveling step (sliding or slipping) in uneven rhythm comprised of a step followed by a small leap to change to the other foot (one foot chases the other)

clogging   A freestyle dance from the Appalachian mountains consisting of double-time stomping and tapping steps while the upper body is held upright; also called flat footing, the shuffling steps while dropping the weight into the floor is the opposite from the emphasis of tap dance where the sounds and taps are pulled out of the floor.

coffee grinder   From Russian folk dance, adopted by break-dancers, a move done in a one leg squat where the free leg circles around the floor as the supporting leg hops over it

Commedia D'ell Arte   Italian professional, improvisational, outdoor theater from the sixteenth century with presentations of popular themes, complex stories, acrobatics, pantomime, and love scenes with stock characters such as Harlequin, Scaramouche, Columbine, and Pantalone (aka Pantaloon), which inspired the characters Punch and Judy, as well as Pierrot and Pierrette

conga   Afro-Cuban dance with accents on the strong beats in 2/4 time; it was popular in the late 1930s and 1940s. Performed in a conga line with each dancer holding onto the waist of the dancer in front, it is a simple three steps and a kick to side or three steps and a chug backward.

contra   A faster version of English country dancing with lots of swinging of one's partner

contredanse   The French adaptation of English country dancing popular during the eighteenth century and done by four couples facing in a square formation

cooch   Sensual dance of swaying and undulating; also known as hootchy-coochy

cotillion   The alternate French spelling is cotilion; this is a French adaptation of the English round for eight done by four couples facing in a square formation and doing complicated figures. The term *cotillion* meant fancy dress ball in the eighteenth century; in the nineteenth century, cotillion became a dance competition; and in the twentieth and twenty-first centuries, the term refers to a formal dance or social dance group.

cotton-eyed Joe   An energetic country and western dance enjoyed in the United States. It uses heel and toe, two-step, kicks, stomps, shuffles, and turns in place or in traveling around the room. It is often done with partners dancing side by side.

country and western dance   A style of couple dancing using primarily a two-step pattern with variations of handholds, sometimes facing partner, sometimes dancing side by side

courante (coronto) Artistocratic dance of the fifteenth to seventeenth centuries characterized by running and gliding steps done by couples in triple time

czárdás/csárdás Traditional vigorous Hungarian folk dances with stomping and slapping of thighs and feet that originated in taverns

dance A series of rhythmic and patterned bodily movements usually performed to music

DanceSport Competitive ballroom dancing with specific rules for performance and choreography and two categories of dancing: Latin (samba, rhumba, cha cha, paso doble, jive) and standard (waltz, Viennese waltz, foxtrot, quickstep, tango)

disco A term for discotheque, a nightclub featuring music and dance to a specialized beat; it was also the fast-paced music and dance of the 1970s, including the hustle and go go dancing characterized by intricate, entwined arm moves and fast-turning footwork.

doo-wop A genre of R&B music with smooth group harmonies in which the singers make nonsense crooning sounds, such as *doo-wop* or *doo-wop, doo-wah* in the chorus

electric boogaloo A style of funk or hip-hop related to popping that uses rolls of the hips, knees, legs, and head; also referred to as electric boogie.

electric slide A line dance of the 1980s–1990s to the song "The Electric Slide" made up of three steps and a tap forward, three steps and a tap backward, four counts of sliding (chassé) right and left, followed by touching the right toe forward, back, to the side before making a quarter turn left and repeating the dance facing the new direction

English country dance Traditional English folk dances with partners in two facing lines (longways) dancing figures of allemande, back-to-back, siding, right or left hand star, slipping, while progressing up or down the set; in America, these dances became contras and squares.

fandango A lively Spanish dance in triple time and performed with castanets or tambourines. The dance begins slowly and tenderly, the rhythm marked by the clack of castanets, the snapping of fingers, and the stomping of feet, the speed gradually increasing to a whirl of exhilaration. It is also the name of a popular English country dance from the eighteenth century.

figure   A series of steps or moves put together to form a specific dance pattern, design or variation, such as *do-si-do, star right,* or *waltz box step*

flamenco   A gypsy dance of Spain with influences from the Moors and the Arabs and characterized by its footwork, which is accompanied by songs, clapping, and guitar

flat footing   Clogging that is largely based on a low-to-the-floor style that emphasizes intricate rhythms and creative percussive dancing

foxtrot   A social dance originated by Harry Fox; it is a standard world-wide ballroom dance, consisting of slow, slow, quick, quick rhythm danced in 2/4 or 4/4 time.

freaking   A slow, grinding version of the twist that became popular in the 1970s; it is associated with a song of the same name and is also called the grind, booty dancing, and the bump and grind.

frug   A dance of hip and arm movements done while standing still. It was born from a dance called the chicken and was used as a change of pace during the twist. From the frug came the swim, the monkey, the dog, the watusi, the jerk, and other novelty dances.

galliard   A bold, lively dance of courtship and coyness consisting of leg thrusts, leaps, swift turns, gliding steps, and foot stamping, especially popular in the court of Elizabeth I

galop   A playful, gliding dance in 2/4 time, originating in Hungary and composed of chassé and hop while making a half turn

gavotte   A fifteenth-century French dance of a gay, hopping quality; it was customary for the leading couple to kiss each other and everyone else in the room at the end of their special "shine."

gigue   A dance characterized by stamping and rapid footwork, small leaps, hops, and kicks; it was popular from the late 1500s to the 1800s

good foot   A 1950s dance invented in New York based on dance movements (mostly walking/strutting) of James Brown while singing "Get On the Good Foot"

gospel   Religious music that expresses praise to God, Christ, or the Holy Spirit and Christian beliefs with origins in Negro spirituals

grand march   Opening of a ball involving all couples to show off their dress and their partner/date. The head couple leads the line of couples down the middle of the hall toward the head of the room where they turn right, the second couple left, third right, and so on. At the foot of the room, two couples join hands to march in a line of four, again splitting alternately right and left; at the foot of the room four couples join hands to march in a line of eight. Then head partners face each other to form an arch, and each couple passes under the arch forming another arch until the last couple has passed through a line of arches.

ha'a   A secret and sacred form of masculine, virile, physical, and precise Hawaiian dance performed by men in outdoor temples to supplicate the gods under direction from a priest for war

habañera   A Cuban folk dance that evolved from the French contredanse in the nineteenth century

hambo   A traditional Swedish couples dance in 3/4 time originating in the late 1800s; it is frequently done during breaks at contra dances.

Harlem Renaissance (1900–1930)   A period during which African-American dancers, singers, and writers in New York City flourished and became popular with white audiences

heavy metal   Rock music with emphasis on the metallic sounds of crashing cymbals, drums, using high amplification, long guitar solos and riffs, and heavy beats associated with "macho man" played by groups such as Led Zeppelin and Deep Purple

hey   A weaving movement in English country dancing where dancers pass right shoulders then left shoulders with the next person and so on in a figure eight pattern

hony-tonk   Club or dance hall catering to the country music scene

hornpipe   A Scottish sailors' dance with leaping, jumping, and leg thrusts and kicks from a squat position

horse ballets   Outdoor equestrian extravaganzas in vogue during the sixteenth and seventeenth centuries, combining dancing and tournaments; dozens of horses were trained to execute steps and complicated geometric figures to music; duels and chases were interspersed with sung choruses; the choreographer was usually the riding and fencing master.

house   A style of electronic music (synthesizers, sequencers, drum machines) that is a mix of soul, funk, and disco forms popular in nightclubs for dancing

hula   Originally a sacred dance of Hawaii to honor Pele (volcano goddess); it utilizes stylized arms, hands, facial expressions, and graceful undulating hips to interpret literature, mythology, genealogy, language, protocol, botany, and craftsmanship.

hully gully   Unstructured dance of the 1960s with origins in black juke joints of the early 1900s; John Belushi does the dance in the film *The Blues Brothers.*

hustle   A style of disco dance from the 1970s; it was influenced by Latin and swing dances in which the simple basic step was elaborated with spins, elaborate arm positions, lifts, and breakaways; it is also a popular line dance.

Jacksonville rounders' dance   Originated in Jacksonville, Florida, "way back" and was well known among semi-rural blacks across the South; a similar dance with many variations had been commonly used in tent show performances; songwriter Perry Bradford rewrote the words in 1919 because *rounder* was a synonym for "pimp" and named it "The Original Black Bottom Dance"; the pimps walk in the earlier dance may be seen in *West Side Story* (hunched shoulders, snapping fingers).

jazz   Initially a form of American music coming principally from New Orleans that has distinct accents and syncopations; later jazz dance was born—a compendium of movement styles that reflect African and European rhythms blended with cultural, historical, and social themes that uses rhythm, line, and dynamics to produce syncopated, percussive movements and accents that is a uniquely American style of dance.

jig   An Irish solo dance using fast, percussive foot movements that evolved in America into patterns of chasing; it is danced in 6/8 time with onlookers cutting out the women or the couple after awhile.

jitterbug   A refined form of Lindy hop originating in the 1930s and using slow, slow, quick, quick rhythm; it was danced to the big band sound popular from World War II into the 1950s.

jive   Fast, lively African-American dance of the 1920s that typified the youth dance craze whose steps later were used in Lindy, boogie woogie, and swing dancing; it is also the European name for the international competitive form of swing dancing.

jota   Spanish folk dance from Aragon in 3/4 or 6/8 rhythm often danced with castanets with varying steps according to the region; rapid footwork, including heel and toe movements, stamping, beaten steps, and fast jumping into a kneeling position followed by swift leaps into the air, demanded speed, strength, and technical skill; it is considered the "father of Spanish dance," originating in Aragon but danced everywhere in Spain.

Kentucky running set   A series of figures for two couples to do, along with various chorus-type figures done either as a square set or as a Sicilian circle rotated so there is an inside couple and an outside couple (called a big set); fast music and brisk smooth walking are used "to run a set," meaning to dance the same figure through for each couple in turn.

krumping   An improvisational, freestyle, rhythmic, coordinated body motion, involving chest popping, comedic fast-paced Charlie Chaplin moves, staccato strides, stumbling, toe dance, torso waves, body jerking, and prancing

lambada   Brazilian dance from the late 1980s that combines the flavor of the samba with the sultry passion of the rhumba; couples dance tightly pressed together and gyrate their hips in synchronized movements.

lambeth walk   A cheeky British novelty dance of the 1930s made popular in the United States by Arthur Murray

landler   A close turning dance from Bavaria in which dancers moved in close embrace and ladies were turned rapidly under the man's hand

limbo   A popular dance to calypso music done at parties where dancers, one at a time, bend backward and scoot forward, knees flexing lower and lower, to pass under a pole or bar until clear

Lindy hop   An original athletic form of swing dancing made famous by dancing couples at the Savoy Ballroom in New York; it was named by "Shorty George" Snowden following Charles Lindbergh's hop (flight) across the Atlantic in 1927.

line dancing   Choreographed moves performed by individual dancers in lines to rock, Latin, or country western music; it originated in the 1980s.

locking   A robotic dance style of move-and-freeze steps giving the dancer a mechanical appearance and done to hip-hop music

longways   A formation used in English country dancing and New England contras in which couples face each other forming a stretched out set with all women on one side facing their men on the other (called "proper") or alternating every other couple switching places (called improper). Every other couple (ones) dances with their neighbor couple (twos), the ones moving down the set (away from the musicians) and the twos progressing up the set. When the twos reach the top, they become ones. In a longways triple minor, figures are danced among three couples, the ones moving down two places to repeat the dance with the next two couples.

macarena   Line dance to a song composed by Los del Rio (1993) in which dancers gesture with their arms, place them on various parts of the body (shoulders, head, hips, buttocks), rotate the hips, and then turn 90 degrees left to repeat the dance

madison   A dance of two parallel lines facing outward with forward and backward steps, shifting weight, and sweeping feet

mambo   A fast Cuban dance style that fuses swing and Cuban music; it was introduced by band leader/composer Perez Prado in 1943 at the Tropicana Hotel in Havana and danced to a quick, quick, slow rhythm.

masque   A dramatic English performance of verse about mythical creatures and Greek gods and goddesses. They were originally sung pieces with dance episodes, the most famous of which combined the talents of British architect Inigo Jones and playwright/poets Ben Jonson and William Shakespeare. Eventually, the importance of music was diminished to the advantage of dance, fusing song, dance, poetry, and drama.

maxixe   An energetic South American dance characterized by swooping body motion. It preceded the samba and used steps and movement from the polka, rhythm of the Cuban habañera, and syncopation from African music. It was introduced by Irene and Vernon Castle and became popular before and after World War I.

mazurka   A wild, exuberant Polish dance that was tamed into a challenging, gallant, and graceful couple dance with a strong accented beat; the basic step is three *pas de basque*, followed by a small jump, clicking the heels together.

measure   A slow, ceremonious English choral dance of the early Renaissance

merengue   A national dance of the Dominican Republic notable for its "limping" sideward movement, dragging one foot to join the other; it was introduced in the United States in the 1950s.

milonga   A Spanish dance that originated in Andalusia; it combines polka and Cuban habañera and was made popular by gauchos in Buenos Aires, where their interpretation of it evolved into tango.

minuet   A carefree and lively dance until adopted by the French court about 1670, where it developed into a slow, graceful, dignified, polite, charming, restrained, and stately dance, elegant in its simplicity and a way to honor women on the dance floor; it is characterized by symmetrical figures, courtly gestures, and elaborate bows and curtsies.

mooche   An African-American dance style with sensuous rotating hips; it was popular in the 1920s and 1930s.

morris dance (also morrisk, morisco)   An English folk dance based on manly strength. It appeared in the fifteenth century and comprised leaping and vigorous arm swinging, dancing in a circle and in a chain, and meeting and interweaving in a succession of figures. Still practiced today, characters include a fool, a boy on a hobby horse, a blackamoor, one dancer in female disguise, and sometimes characters from the legend of Robin Hood.

new wave   Experimental music of the 1970s combining the disco sound with electronic music and pop music of the 1960s

one-step   A dance consisting entirely of single steps to the beat without any change in rhythm; it was danced to the popular music of World War I.

pas de basque   Dance step consisting of a side leap followed by a forward step with the back foot closing to the other foot; it can also be done stepping to the side. Variations on its form occur in classical ballet, Scottish dancing, and Irish dancing.

pavane   A dignified court dance characterized by strutting with pomp and stateliness and popular in the fifteenth century

peabody   The name for quickstep in the United States in the 1920s; it was characterized by a crossing of the man's right foot behind the left and woman's right foot in front of the left.

polka   A Czech peasant dance in 2/4 time of three steps, with a hop on the fourth beat while turning; it became a popular ballroom dance for couples in the mid-nineteenth century and is still popular today.

polonaise   Dignified Polish processional dance of couples walking around the dance hall to music in 3/4 time, pausing to bow to other couples

popping   A movement developed in the 1970s from *locking*. Popping describes the sequential movement of the joints by break-dancers to appear as though an electric current is passing through the dancer; it is also known as the electric boogie.

powwow   A Native American gathering, originally referring to Native American medicine or curing ceremonies, then to a "council" or gathering to talk, especially for political reasons. Originating in the plains as a social celebration of Indian life, it is now a secular event featuring group singing and social dancing by men, women, and children.

promenade   A processional walking step with couples side by side

punk   Genre of fast, hard-edged music, usually of short songs, stripped-down instrumentation, and often political, antiestablishment lyrics developed in the mid-1970s

quadrille   A French social dance popular in the nineteenth century and danced by two to twelve couples in a square with couples facing couples. It was danced in five sections, each in a different time signature. Consisting of a series of dance figures, the most frequently used was the "flirtation" figure in which the man danced with each woman in turn. It is considered the forerunner of American square dancing. The most popular, Lancers quadrille, was named for a type of calvary that fought with lances.

quickstep   A fast variation of the foxtrot (54–56 measures per minute), which has quick hopping and Charleston steps set in with the smoother gliding figures

ragtime   March tempo music for piano or band with a syncopated or "ragged" melody that was the basis for jazz music, popular from 1897–1918

rave   Genre of music using synthesizers to create a trancelike sound (chill-out music); it is also a term used to describe an all-night dance, usually in a nightclub, where rave music is predominant.

reel   A lively, light, rapid, leaping dance for two or more energetic couples in which intricate footwork alternated with an interweaving pattern. The reel originated around 1750 in Scotland, although Irish dancing masters were the ones who fully developed it. It is also the name of a figure in which partners swing each other in the center of a longways, then swing the opposite sex on the side, returning to the partner and working their way down the set in this manner.

réverénce　A formal courtesy to honor the king and queen and one's partner. The bow or curtsy had various versions according to the century: *sink and rise demi plié* (knee bend) from fourth position with straight back (fifteenth and sixteenth centuries); *demi plié* with heels together and toes rotated at 45 degrees, spine straight (seventeenth and eighteenth centuries); and *demi plié* on back leg with one foot pointed in front and the body leaning forward from the hips (eighteenth and nineteenth centuries, also the informal bow in the eighteenth century).

rhumba/rumba　Originally a Cuban marriage dance; the ballroom form that came to the United States in 1933 uses the Cuban son, guaracha, and danzon. Many rhumba movements and actions, which appear to be erotic, actually depict simple farm tasks—tossing seed, shoeing a mare, courtship of rooster and hen. The straightening of the leg taking weight causes the hips to sway from side to side in what is known as "Cuban motion." The rhythm is quick, quick, slow.

rigaudon/rigadoon　A lively seventeenth-century French Baroque folk dance for couples. In Scotland, the seventeenth-century *rigaudon* was the dance performed by Highland soldiers on the cross blades of swords with lightness, strength, and catlike use of the feet; it is also the name of a jumping step.

rock 'n' roll　Popular music of the 1950s and 1960s played by artists such as Bill Haley and the Comets and Elvis Presley; it was danced to by their teenage fans.

round dances　Circular choral dances of the Middle Ages, couple dances in the 1800s, and folk dances in America, which became barn dances, square dances, and big circle dances

salsa　The name for Latin music with roots in Cuban culture and jazz textures developed by Puerto Rican musicians in New York; the dance structure is a repackaging of mambo patterns. It reached its height of popularity at end of twentieth century.

saltarello　A light, fast, jumping dance enjoyed by commoners in the fifteenth and sixteenth centuries; it included gesture (acting) and pantomime.

samba　A Brazilian dance in syncopated 4/4 meter. It was introduced in 1917, adopted as a ballroom dance by Brazilian society in 1930, and introduced in the United States in 1939 by Carmen Miranda. The style is three bouncing steps forward and back with rocking hips.

sarabande   A wild, sexually suggestive dance done by couples; it was considered vulgar and indecent at the beginning of the sixteenth century but popular at court by the seventeenth century.

schottische   A German dance derived from the waltz and done in 2/4 time with a step and skip, similar to the polka; later, in folk dance, it consisted of three running steps and a hop done in 4/4 time.

setting   A step in country dancing where couples face each other spring lightly to the right side, and then quickly transfer weight to left and back to right, and then repeat to the left side

shag   A popular dance in the late 1930s; along with the jitterbug and the Lindy, it was done to up-tempo swing or foxtrot music and was composed of a sideward step and hop, causing a rocking motion. Originally called the "flea-hop" in New Jersey and the "sugar foot" in North Carolina, Arthur Murray invented his own version called Arthur Murray shag.

shimmy   A vigorous vibratory shaking of the shoulders made famous by Gilda Grey and Mae West

shim sham shimmy   A four-step tap dance performed at the end of an evening of Lindy consisting of a shuffle step, the push and crossover, the tack Annie, and the half break

shorty George   A walking step from the 1930s and 1940s where the feet swivel while the fingers point up and down

shuffle   Loose-limbed brushing and shuffling movements developed by African Americans as part of "levee dancing"; when used in minstrel shows, the dance became a parody of the way white people thought blacks moved.

Sir Roger de Coverly   An English country longways dance for three couples that is believed to be the basis for the Virginia reel; a simple dance everyone could do, it was sometimes danced at the end of the evening to finish the ball or assembly.

slow drag   An end-of-evening low down blues dance originating in the 1890s in New Orleans in which dancers hung on each other, shuffling their feet now and then while undulating and writhing their bodies

soul   Combination of rhythm and blues (R&B), doo-wop, and gospel

square dance   An American folk dance with four couples forming a square, the heads and sides "visiting" each other while dancing figures announced by a caller

step dancing   A form of Irish dance—combining artistry, grace, and physical ability—that went with Irish immigrants and Irish missionaries wherever they traveled, including North America, Australia, New Zealand, Brittany France, Singapore, and Africa; it reached the height of popularity with the show *Riverdance.*

stepping   A rhythmic, unison style of street dance made popular by African-American fraternities in the 1990s

strathspey   A stately Scottish country dance in 4/4 time for six to eight couples, usually followed by a reel; there are nearly 700 strathspeys.

stroll   A dance of the late 1950s and early 1960s in which couples danced in a double line, one couple at a time "strolling" up the middle to the other end

Suzy Q   An African-American jazz move from the 1920s, often done in tap dance; in it, the knees swivel in one direction while the arms swing in counter direction.

swing   A blend of Lindy, jitterbug, ragtime, jazz, and blues and the music that accompanies them

sword dance   Male folk dance performed over two swords or a sword and scabbard crossed on the ground; originally sword dances served as military training. There are also hilt-and-point sword dances where the dancers are linked together by holding the hilt of their sword and the point of another's sword. The rapper sword dance from northeast England involves five dancers using short, flexible, two-handled swords (rappers) to form a chain, while the long sword dance uses rigid metal or wooden swords.

tango   A social dance in 2/4 time, originating in Spain but developed in Argentina from the Cuban habañera del café and the milonga. It was made respectable by Vernon and Irene Castle before World War I. Its ballroom form has a slow, slow, quick, quick, slow rhythm. In the Argentine tango (arrabalero), the dancer interprets the music spontaneously without any predetermined slows or quicks, and both male and female make small kicks around and between the partner's legs responding to both legato and staccato musical phrasing.

tarantella   Originally a wild jumping dance of Italy thought to cure the bite of the spider; it became a flirting folk dance of couples before it faded to a milder version done for amusement by lower- and middle- class girls using tambourines and castanets.

techno   A genre of dance music using electronic synthesizer combined with disco beat popular in the late 1980s

tin pan alley   A real alley in New York City where publishing houses sold a mixture of many musical styles—blues, jazz, musical scores, and ragtime; it has come to symbolize the era of songwriting when publishers pitched their music to singers, orchestra leaders, dancers, and comedians and began selling sheet music to the public.

tranky doo   A series of jazz, Lindy, and big apple steps choreographed by Pepsi Bethel in the Savoy Ballroom during the 1940s and danced to "Tuxedo Junction" or Ella Fitzgerald's "Dipsy Doodle"

triumph   A combination of verse, music, and dance that became the standard manner of welcoming visiting dignitaries to court in the sixteenth and seventeenth centuries

truckin'   An African-American move of shuffling while shaking the index finger of one hand above the head; it was popular in 1937 and was infused into the Lindy hop.

turkey trot   One of the first animal dances done from 1895 to 1910 to fast ragtime music (such as Scott Joplin's "Maple Leaf Rag"); it consisted of sideward hopping steps embellished with scissors-like flicks of the feet and rapid trotting actions with abrupt stops, and occasional flapping of the arms. Its popularity resulted in part from its being denounced by the Vatican.

twist   A fast, frantic dance with no real steps in which dancers rotate hips and knees in a twisting fashion. It can be done in a group or with a partner, but rarely do dancers touch. It was popularized on *American Bandstand* to the music of Chubby Checker.

two-step   A simple marching dance, more or less double quick time with a skip in each step, made popular by John Philip Sousa's music "Washington Post March" in 1891; the Texas two-step uses timing of quick, quick, slow, slow.

varsouvienne　An Americanized version of traditional varsouvienne from Warsaw, Poland, made popular as a ballroom dance by Arthur Murray in 1940; it is also the name of a side-by-side position with left hands held in front of the couple's waists, hands crossed with partner and man's right arm over lady's shoulder holding her right hand

vaudeville　A variety show or revue of 10 to 15 acts—comedy, juggling, singing, dancing, and magic—that was the primary form of popular entertainment in Europe and America in the early twentieth century

Viennese waltz　A swift dance in 3/4 time with a strong first beat accent with a smaller step, greater speed, and smoother, compact turns than that of the waltz

Virginia reel　A popular folk dance done in longways formation; it was derived from the early English country dance Sir Roger de Coverly.

vogueing　A vernacular dance form originating in clubs in New York City; it imitates fashion model poses.

volta　A forerunner of the waltz originating in Germany and brought to the French court by way of Italy by the Count of Sault in 1556; it was the first dance in which partners danced in close embrace (rather than alongside), the man turning his partner around several times and then lifting her in a high turning jump in the air, using his thigh as a rudder under her thigh.

waltz　A turning dance in triple time that became fashionable without the sanction of court, dancing masters, or France; it was popularized by composers such as Johann and Richard Strauss. In the waltz, couples rotate around each other as they circle around the dance floor.

watusi　Fad dance in 1962 popular with the subculture surfing crowd in which the arms flail up and down while the feet swivel, and the head bobs danced to the song "Wah-Watusi"

zumba　A twenty-first-century form of low-impact aerobic dancing to Latin music where fast and slow rhythms and resistance training are combined

zydeco　A Cajun/Creole-style dance from southwest Louisiana; it uses a syncopated slow, quick, quick pattern and foot brushes, kicks, and toe and heel taps.

BIBLIOGRAPHY

Arbeau, Thoinot. *Orchesography*. Trans. C.W. Beaumont. New York: Dance Horizons, 1965.

Baker, William Spohn. *Washington After the Revolution*. Philadelphia: J.B. Lippincott, 1892.

Beauchamp, William. "Notes on Onondaga Dances." *Journal of American Folklore* VI (1893): 181–184.

Bond, Chrystelle T. "A Chronicle of Dance in Baltimore, 1780–1814," *Dance Perspectives* 17, no. 66 (Summer 1976) New York: Dance Perspectives Foundation.

Bouchet, Guillaume. "Notes sur la vie privée a la Renaissance." *La Revue de Paris* 3 (1896).

Capture, George Horse. *Powwow*. Cody, WY: Buffalo Bill Historic Museum, 1989.

Catlin, George. *Letters and Notes on the Manners and Customs of the North American Indians*. 2 vols. Edinburgh: John Grant, 1926.

Childe Dorr, Rheta Louise. *What Eight Million Women Want*. Boston: Small, Maynard, 1910; New York: Kraus Reprint, 1971.

"Colored Theatre Opens: The Old Bijou Shows the Darktown Follies of 1914," *The New York Times*, June 16, 1914, pp. 9.

Cresswell, Nicholas. *The Journal of Nicholas Cresswell, 1774–1777*. New York: Dial Press, 1924.

Custis, George Washington Parke. *Recollections and Private Memoirs*. New York: Derby & Jackson, 1860.

Dawson, Jim. *Rock Around the Clock: The Record That Started the Rock Revolution!* San Francisco: Backbeat Books, 2005.

De Valcourt, Robert. *The Illustrated Manners Book: A Manual of Good Behavior and Polite Accomplishments*. New York: Leland Clay & Co., 1855.

Driver, Ian. *A Century of Dance: A Hundred Years of Musical Movement, from Waltz to Hip Hop*. London: Bounty Books, 2006.

Durang, John. *The Memoir of John Durang: American Actor, 1785–1816*. Ed. Alan S. Downer. Pittsburgh, PA: University of Pittsburgh Press, 1966.

Ehrenreich, Barbara. *Dancing in the Streets*. New York: Henry Holt and Company, 2006.

Emery, Lynne F. *Black Dance in the United States, 1619–1970*. Palo Alto, CA: National Press Books, 1972.

Enomoto, Kekoa Catherine. *Guide to the Islands—Hula and Chant*. Aiea, HI: Island Heritage, 1998.

Giordano, Ralph G. *Social Dancing in America: A History and Reference, 1607–1900*. Westport, CT: Greenwood Press, 2007.

Hemoni. "To Parents." *Times and Seasons* 4 (April 1, 1844): 486.

Highwater, Jamake. *Ritual of the Wind: North American Indian Ceremonies, Music, and Dances*. New York: Viking Press, 1977.

Hilton, Wendy. *Dance of Court and Theater: The French Noble Style, 1690–1725*. Hillsdale, NY: Pendragon Press, 1981.

Hoop Dancing and World Citizenship: Meet Kevin Locke. One Country vol. 8 no. 2 (July–September 1996), Available online at http://www.onecountry.org/oc82/oc8208as.htm.

Kassing, Gayle. *History of Dance: An Interactive Arts Approach*. Champaign, IL: Human Kinetics, 2007.

Keller, Kate Van Winkle, and Charles Cyril Hendrickson. *George Washington: A Biography in Social Dance*. Sandy Hook, CT: The Henderson Group, 1998.

Kirsten, Lincoln. *Dance: A Short History of Classical Theatrical Dancing*. Princeton, NJ: Dance Horizons Books, 1977.

Lee, William Storrs. *The Yankees of Connecticut*, New York: Henry Holt, 1957.

Malnig, Julie, ed. *Ballroom, Boogie, Shimmy Sham, Shake: A Social and Popular Dance Reader*. Chicago and Urbana: University of Illinois Press, 2009.

Manning, Frankie, and Cynthia R. Millman. *Frankie Manning: Ambassador of Lindy Hop*. Philadelphia: Temple University Press, 2007.

Native American Dance: Ceremonies and Social Traditions. Washington, DC: National Museum of the American Indian National Powwow, 2005.

Needham, Maureen. *I See America Dancing, Selected Reading 1685–2000*. Chicago and Urbana: University of Illinois Press, 2002.

Nevell, Richard. *A Time to Dance: American Country Dancing from Hornpipes to Hot Hash*. New York: St. Martin's Press, 1977.

Page, Ralph. "A History of Square Dance in America." *Focus on Dance: VIII, Dance Heritage*, 23–32. Washington, DC: National Dance Association, 1971.

Partsch-Bergsohn, Isa. *Early Dance: From the Greeks to the Renaissance.* Pennington, NJ: Dance Horizons Video, 1995.

Payton, Colleen M. "Traditional Native Dance Past & Present." *Native Peoples Magazine*, vol. XIX (Sept./Oct. 2006): 46–49.

Prynne, William. *Histrio-Mastix: The Player's Scourge; or, Actor's Tragedy*, 1632, Norton Anthology of English Literature, Available online at www.wwnorton.com/college/english/nael/17century/topic_3/prynne.htm.

Quirey, Belinda, *May I Have the Pleasure? The Story of Popular Dancing.* London: Dance Books, 1987.

Radziwill, Princess. *They Knew the Washingtons.* Indianapolis, IN: Bobbs-Merrill Company, 1926.

Richmond Dancing Assemblies [manuscript collection, 1790s], Virginia Historical Society, Richmond.

Roan, Carol. *Clues to American Dance.* Philadelphia: Starrhill Press, 1931.

Roberts, Cokie. *Founding Mothers: The Women Who Raised Our Nation.* New York: William Morrow, 2004.

Sachs, Curt. *World History of the Dance.* New York: W.W. Norton & Company, 1963.

Schoolcraft, Henry Rowe. *The Indian in His Wigwam or Characteristics of the Red Race of America.* New York: W.H. Graham, 1848.

Stearns, Marshall and Jean Stearns. *Jazz Dance: the Story of American Vernacular Dance*, New York: MacMillan, 1968.

Stegeman, John F., and Janet A. Stegeman. *Caty, a Biography of Catherine Littlefield Greene.* Athens: University of Georgia Press, 1977.

Stephenson, Richard M., and Joseph Iaccarino. *The Complete Book of Ballroom Dancing.* Garden City, New York: Doubleday & Company, 1980.

Stiles, Henry R. *Ancient Windsor, Connecticut.* 2 vols. Hartford, CT: Lockwood & Brainard, 1891.

Van Cleef, Joy. "Rural Felicity: Social Dance in 18th Century Connecticut." *Dance Perspectives* 17, no. 65 (Spring 1976). New York: Dance Perspectives Foundation.

Waxman, Donald, and Wendy Hilton. *A Dance Pageant: Renaissance and Baroque Keyboard Dances.* Boston: Galaxy Music Corporation, 1992.

Widstoe, John A., ed. *The Discourses of Brigham Young.* Salt Lake City, UT: Deseret Book, 1925.

Wilson, George E. *Wilson's Ball-room Guide and Call Book, or, Dancing Self-Taught*. New York: Excelsior, 1884.

Wilson, Thomas. *An Analysis of Country Dancing*, 3rd ed. London: J. S. Dickson, 1811.

Wood, Melusine. *Historical Dances: 12th to 19th Centuries, Their Manner of Performance and Their Place in the Social Life of the Times*. London: Dance Books, 1952.

FURTHER RESOURCES

BOOKS

Aloff, Mindy. *Dance Anecdotes: Stories from the Worlds of Ballet, Broadway, the Ballroom, and Modern Dance*. New York: Oxford University Press, 2006.

Barrére, Dorothy B., Mary Kawena Pukui, and Marion Kelly. *HULA: Historical Perspectives*. Honolulu, HI: Bishop Museum Press, 1980.

Brissenden, Alan. *Shakespeare and the Dance*. Atlantic Highlands, NJ: Humanities Press, 1981.

Cohen, Selma Jean, ed. *International Encyclopedia of Dance*. 6 vols. New York: Oxford University Press, 1998.

Emery, Lynne Fauley. *Black Dance in the United States from 1619 to 1970*. Palo Alto, CA: National Press Books, 1972.

Fallon, Dennis J., ed. *Encores for Dance*. Washington, DC: National Dance Association, 1978.

Fletcher, Iran Kyrle, Selma Jean Cohen, and Roger Lonsdale. *Famed for Dance: Essays on the Theory and Practice of Theatrical Dancing in England, 1660–1740*. New York: New York Public Library, 1960.

Harris, Jane A., et al. *Dance a While: Handbook for Folk, Square, Contra, and Social Dance*. Boston: Allyn and Bacon, 2000.

Hayes, Elizabeth R. *The Evolution of Visual, Literary, and Performing Arts: From Tribal Cultures through the Middle Ages*. Herriman, UT: Blue Ribbon Books, 2004.

Heth, Charlotte, ed. *Native American Dance: Ceremonies and Social Traditions*. Washington, DC: Smithsonian Institution, 1993.

Highwater, Jamake. *Ritual of the Wind: North American Indian Ceremonies, Music, and Dances*. New York: The Viking Press, 1977.

Imel, E. Carmen, ed. *Focus on Dance VIII: Dance Heritage*. Washington, DC: National Dance Association, 1977.

Lamb, Andrew. *150 Years of Popular Musical Theatre*. New Haven, CT: Yale University Press, 2000.

Laubin, Reginald and Gladys Laubin. *Indian Dances of North America: Their Importance to Indian Life*. Norman: University of Oklahoma Press, 1977.

Lihs, Harriet. *Appreciating Dance: A Guide to the World's Liveliest Art*. Hightstown, NJ: Princeton Book Company, 2002.

Mails, Thomas E. *Dancing in the Paths of the Ancestors*. New York: Marlowe & Company, 1993.

Martin, Carol. *Dance Marathons*. Jackson, MS: University Press of Mississippi, 1994.

McBride, James. "Hip Hop Planet." *National Geographic*, April 2007. Available online at http://ngm.nationalgeographic.com/2007/04/hip-hop-planet/mcbride-text.html.

McGowan, Margaret M. *Dance in the Renaissance: European Fashion, French Obsession*. New Haven, CT: Yale University Press, 2008.

Newman, Cathy, "Shall We Dance?" *National Geographic*, July 2006, Available online at http://ngm.nationalgeographic.com/2006/07/dance/newman-text.html.

Sharp, Cecil. *The Morris Book, Part I*. London: Novello, 1912.

Stewart, Travis (Trav S.D.). *No Applause—Just Throw Money: The Book That Made Vaudeville Famous*. New York: Faber and Faber, 2005.

Thorpe, Edward. *Black Dance*. Woodstock, NY: The Overlook Press, 1989.

Weaver, John. *Orchesography: and A Small Treatise of Time and Cadence in Dancing*. London: 1706 (New York: Dance Horizons [Reprint], 1971.)

Zimmer, Elizabeth, and Mindy N. Levine, eds. *Dancing in the Americas*. New York: Arts Connection, 1983.

WEB SITES

Breakdancing

http://www.npr.org/programs/morning/features/patc/breakdancing/

NPR's site explains the evolution of break dancing.

Dance Heritage Coalition

http://www.danceheritage.org

This site offers an alliance of major dance collections, formed to document and preserve America's dance history.

Dances of Colonial America

http://www.colonialmusic.org/Resource/Danctyps.htm

The Colonial Music Institute's site about dance in the American colonies includes information about the reel, minuet, cotillion, and country dances.

Smithsonian National Museum of the American Indian

http://www.AmericanIndian.si.edu

The Smithsonian's site includes events and exhibits on Native American dance.

Society of Dance History Scholars

http://www.sdhs.org

This organization advances the field of dance studies through research, publication, performance, and outreach to audiences across the arts, humanities, and social sciences.

Western Social Dance

http://memory.loc.gov/ammem/dihtml/diessay0.html

This site gathers information on Western social dance, from the late 1400s to early 1900s.

VIDEOGRAPHY

500 Years of Social Dance, 6 vols., Dancetime Publications, 2002.

Country Corners, the Tradition of the Contra Dance in New England, produced by Robert Fiore and Richard Nevel.

Dance Black America (shows Mama Lu Parks dancers doing the Lindy hop), Dance Horizons, 1986.

Dancing, Volumes I–VIII, Kultur, 1993.

Early Dances: From the Greeks to the Renaissance, by Isa Partsch-Gergsohn, Dance Horizons Video, 1995.

Tango, Geneva Grand Theatre Ballet, View Video, 1987.

The Spirit Moves: A History of Black Social Dance on Film, 1900–1986, Dancetime Publications, 2008.

They Shoot Horses, Don't They? (movie about dance marathons), dir. Sydney Pollack, 1970.

PICTURE CREDITS

PAGE

INDEX

ABOUT THE AUTHOR

Author **Karen Lynn Smith** is Professor and Director of the Dance Program at Washington College in Chestertown, MD. She has a BS in Dance and an MA in Physical Education from the University of Maryland and is a certified instructor in Pilates mat and apparatus. She has received awards from regional, national, and international professional organizations. Karen was director of the Dance Commission of ICHPER•SD (the International Council for Health, Physical Education, Recreation, Sport, and Dance) from 1994–2004 and received the 1995 ICHPER•SD Distinguished Scholar Award in Dance Education. She has taught hundreds of workshops and master classes in jazz, ballet, modern dance, yoga, Pilates, and stretching and has presented scholarly papers on Native American dance, dance curricula, nutrition, flexibility, alignment, and somatics locally, nationally, and internationally, including seven International Dance Council (CID-UNESCO) World Congresses in Greece and Spain, the World Dance Alliance Global Assembly (Toronto), and six ICHPER-SD World Congresses in Ireland, Korea, Japan, the United States, Egypt, and Taiwan. She is a founder and the Executive Director of the Maryland Council for Dance, a consultant to the Maryland State Department of Education, and serves as chair of the Advisory Committee of the national Dance Honor Society—Nu Delta Alpha. She has published more than 50 research papers in journals and conference proceedings, authored a chapter on Pilates in the textbook *Teaching Cues for Secondary Physical Education and Sport* (2007), and is co-authoring a book on Pilates for golf. She is the 2010 recipient of the Honor Award for service to the professions from the American Alliance for Health, Physical Education, Recreation, and Dance (AAHPERD).

ABOUT THE CONSULTING EDITOR

Consulting editor **Elizabeth A. Hanley** is associate professor emerita of Kinesiology at the Pennsylvania State University. She holds a BS in physical education from the University of Maryland and an MS in physical education from Penn State, where she taught such courses as modern dance, figure skating, international folk dance, square and contra dance, and ballroom dance. She is the founder and former director of the Penn State International Dance Ensemble and has served as the coordinator of the dance workshop at the International Olympic Academy in Olympia, Greece.